THE
FINAL
SEASON

BILL PARCELLS

with Will McDonough

THE FINAL SEASON

My Last Year As Head Coach in the NFL

William Morrow

An Imprint of HarperCollins*Publishers*

Acknowledgment is made to reprint the excerpt from *The Coaches* by Bill Libby. Copyright © 1972 by Henry Regnery Publishing. All rights reserved. Reprinted by special permission of Regnery Publishing, Inc., Washington, D.C.

Photographs on pages 32, 40, 50, 58, 68, 76, 100, 128, 164, 188, 196, 216, 224 copyright © Bill Lenahan; 2, 26, 86, 92, 108, 120, 136, 146, 156, 172, 180, 206 copyright © Al Pereira.

HarperCollins books may be purchased for educational, business, or sales promotional use. For information please write: Special Markets Department, HarperCollins Publishers, Inc., 10 East 53rd Street, New York, NY 10022.

FIRST EDITION

Designed by Joseph Rutt

Printed on acid-free paper

Library of Congress Cataloging-in-Publication Data

Parcells, Bill
    The final season : my last year as head coach in the NFL / Bill Parcells with Will McDonough.—1st ed.
        p. cm.
    ISBN 0-688-17491-4 (alk. paper)
    1. Parcells, Bill—Diaries. 2. Football coaches—New York (State)—New York—Diaries. 3. Football—Coaching—New York (State)—New York—Diaries. I. McDonough, Will. II. Title.

GV939.P35 P37 2000
796.332'092—dc21
    [B]   00-055028

00 01 02 03 04 ❖/QW 10 9 8 7 6 5 4 3 2 1

This book is dedicated to my favorite people, coaches. Several years ago I was reading a book about coaching and copied the following essay which I kept with me over the years in my desk drawer and had it laminated to preserve it. It says for me what I feel in my heart about coaching.

From *The Coaches* by Bill Libby

He is called "coach." . . . It is a difficult job, and there is no clear way to succeed in it. One cannot copy another who is a winner, for there seems to be some subtle, secret chemistry of personality that enables a person to lead successfully, and no one really knows what it is. Those who have succeeded and those who have failed represent all kinds— young and old, inexperienced and experienced, hard and soft, tough and gentle, good-natured and foul-tempered, proud and profane, articulate and inarticulate, even dedicated and casual. Most are dedicated, some more than others, but dedication alone is not enough. Some are smarter than others, but intelligence is not enough. All want to win, but some want to win more than others, and just wanting is not enough in any event. Even winning is often not enough. Losers almost always get fired, but winners get fired, too. . . .

He is out in the open being judged publicly almost every day or night for six, seven, or eight months a year by those who may or may not be qualified to judge him. And every victory and every defeat is recorded constantly in print or on the air and periodically totaled up.

The coach has no place to hide. He cannot just let the job go for a while or do a bad job and assume no one will notice as most of us can. He cannot satisfy everyone. Seldom can he even satisfy very many. Rarely can he even satisfy himself. If he wins once, he must win the next time, too. . . .

They plot victories, suffer defeats, endure criticism from within and without. . . . They neglect their families, travel endlessly, and live alone in a spotlight surrounded by others.

Theirs may be the worst profession—unreasonably demanding and insecure and full of unrelenting pressures. Why do they put up with it? . . . Having seen them hired and hailed as geniuses at gaudy party-like press conferences and having seen them fired with pat phrases such as "fool" or "incompetent," I have [sympathized with] them. Having seen them exultant in victory and depressed by defeat. Having seen some broken by the job and others die from it, [one is moved to admire them and hope that someday the world will learn to understand them].

PREFACE

When I agreed to do this book, it was supposed to be the story of a year in the life of a coach, dealing with the day-to-day business and all of the pressures that come with the job as he goes through a winning season. The season didn't turn out that way. Our chance for a Super Bowl vanished in the first week when the team was decimated by injury.

To do the book after that was painful, especially in the form of a diary, which we decided in advance was the way to go to give a true picture of my life for twelve months. It was not easy to sit down one morning a week, throwing out thoughts in a stream of consciousness. I'm not good at losing. I never have been. I don't deal with it well, and you'll read that. I don't feel like I held anything back. If I was down, I was down. I didn't try to hide it. I wish there were more upsides to this season, but there weren't.

Besides losing, I had to deal with my own life and my career, to decide whether I wanted to stay in coaching or not. After a lot of difficult soul-searching I decided to retire from coaching. As I write this, it's the final week of April in the year 2000. I still can't pull the trigger on what I want to do with the rest of my life.

Walking away from coaching, or playing, or being involved in the National Football League is not easy. All of us are competitors, or else we wouldn't be in this business. So we know that when we finally have the heart to say "that's it," we better be right, because it means the days of competing are over, and when you've been doing something your whole life, it's not easy to accept.

Ever since I was a kid I loved to play ball. Before high school my family lived in a suburban community—Ashbrook Heights, New Jersey. I used to play right out in front of my house with the other kids in the neighborhood, where the streets were our fields. We played pickup games of baseball, football, and basketball, and I loved them all. About the time I went to high school, we moved to a place called Oradell, New Jersey, and I went to River Dell High School, which was a big break for me. That's where I met Mickey Corcoran, who coached me in basketball, and to this day is still one of my best friends. I think he picked up right away that I had a passion for sports and might even be the kind of kid who could coach someday. He loved to coach, and by watching him and playing for him, I had it in the back of my head even in high school that someday I might do it.

I played all three sports in high school, but baseball was my favorite. I was a catcher. In my senior year of high school and after my freshman year at Colgate, I had a chance to sign a pro contract with the Phillies. I wanted to, but my dad didn't want me to sign. He said I should go to college. I attended Colgate and played football and baseball there, but I didn't like it. When the Phillies offered me another contract, and my dad again wouldn't allow me to sign, I rebelled and left Colgate. I didn't see any sense in staying there if I wasn't going on to a baseball career.

So I decided to play football. I transferred to Wichita. In high school I had played quarterback on offense and linebacker on defense. In college I played a combination of linebacker on defense and tight end on offense. In my final year I played offensive line. The Detroit Lions gave me a shot and invited me to their training camp. This was 1964, and Judy and I were already married with one kid, and another on the way, so I needed the money.

In the meantime, Dean Prior, one of our assistant coaches at Wichita, had just taken a head coaching job with Hastings, a small

Division III football college in Nebraska. He offered me a coaching job with him, but I wasn't sure what was going to happen with the Lions. I thought I did real well in camp. So I explained my situation to head coach George Wilson and asked him what were my chances of making the team. He just put me off.

"Play this final preseason game and then I'll let you know," he said. I called Judy and we talked it over. I stayed and played. Still Wilson wouldn't tell me anything, so I took the job in Hastings, and that started my coaching career. I was lucky. I loved it right away. Being at such a small school forced me to learn from the ground up. I cut the grass on the field, I helped build lockers, I washed the equipment after practice, and I couldn't get enough of it.

A lot has happened since then, but my love for the game has never changed. And now I was at a point where I didn't want to be taken away from the sidelines boots first. A few years ago Phil Simms was struggling to make a decision on whether he wanted to play again or not. I told him not to end up a boots-first guy, someone they have to drag away because he just doesn't want it to end. There's something about the game that is addictive. It becomes a way of life. It's in your blood.

Just a month or so after the 1999 season was over, Dan Marino, a player I have a lot of respect for, was trying to figure out what he wanted to do. A mutual friend asked me to give him a call.

Dan knew the Dolphins didn't want him back, and he wanted my ideas on whether he should take a shot with Minnesota for one last year, if I thought he had enough left to do it. We talked about many things, but it boiled down to this: I told him, "If it's your heart that wants to play, go back and play. But if it's your ego, don't."

We had a long conversation and we learned that we are alike. We both love sports. He told me what it was like being a kid in Pittsburgh going down to watch Pitt games. I told him about my father taking me to Giants games when I was young. Both of us played other sports.

Everybody in pro sports is different, yet the same. We come from all kinds of backgrounds and different cultures, but when it comes to competing, there are no differences. And if you have been around long enough and are successful enough, then money is not an issue. It wasn't with Simms or Marino, and it's not with me.

There is a certain feeling of power walking to midfield and putting on the headsets, waiting for the battle to begin. There is a special feeling for players when they charge out of the dressing room in their uniforms.

I'll guarantee you that if you went to the great coaches and great players of the past and said they could be young for one more day and do anything they wanted to do, all of them would want to be involved in one more Super Bowl game.

That's what I wanted in 1999. It didn't happen. I can still walk away satisfied that I gave it my best shot, but it doesn't make up for the way the season turned out.

THE
FINAL
SEASON

INTRODUCTION
APRIL 1, 1999

I'm fifty-eight years old, and I don't intend to be coaching when I'm sixty. At least that's the way I'm thinking at this point in time. Toward the end of the 1998 season, when we made a good run at winning the AFC and getting to the Super Bowl, I began to think it was time to retire.

Coming down the stretch we had some tough, pressurized games, where we were working on adrenaline more than anything else. The staff was tired, and the coaching was hard, and it was tough for me and the team to find the right balance as we fought for the playoffs. Keeping the football team honed is part of the reason why my teams over the years have generally improved during the last part of the season.

It's not easy to find the right balance. I have to work them hard enough to keep them sharp, but not too hard. What's enough? How much should I give them to pump them up and to keep them at a tough level? When do you cut practices short and give them a break to rejuvenate themselves?

As for me, I've got a heart condition and a weight problem. Working on adrenaline alone isn't good for me. In fact, if I have trouble, more arrhythmia than I am comfortable with, it comes when I'm exhausted. At the start of the season in recent years, I have had my weight down and my endurance up. My weight is

With Leon Hess at the 1997 press conference announcing my coming to the New York Jets.

nowhere near as low as it should be, but it is a lot better than it is toward the end of the season. I work out hard through the spring, training camp, and the halfway mark of the season, then the crunch comes. I start to eat too much. My weight goes up. I get tired. I don't work out as much. I start asking myself, "What the hell am I doing this for?" I don't need the money. I don't need the fame. And I certainly don't need to feel as lousy as I do sometimes, trying to take a team down the stretch and into the tournament. The pressure just beats the hell out of me, and it takes a long time to recover.

After we lost to Denver in the 1998 AFC championship, I was just about as low as I could get. I really thought we had a chance at beating them, then doing something in the Super Bowl. We had beaten Atlanta during the regular season, so I would have liked our chances in that one, but it didn't work out that way.

We ended the season by beating Seattle, Miami, Buffalo, and the Patriots, who were all fighting for a playoff spot just like we were. Every game was tough. We beat Seattle at the end of a home game on a controversial call. Then we had to go to Miami for a Sunday night game, have a short week, and play in Buffalo the following Saturday. It doesn't get any tougher than that. Two divisional opponents on the road with the division up for grabs. I hate to play night games on the road. You sit around all day waiting and it eats you up. When I get nervous, I'm a compulsive eater, and there's no way I can keep my weight under control when this happens. I lose energy. It doesn't take long. In two or three weeks my condition can go from good to bad.

That happened to me this time. Miami was a grinder. The game was up for grabs until the last two minutes, when we made a great play to win it. I've always said that those are the greatest victories of all, winning on the road, in a big game, before a packed house.

People always ask if the two Super Bowl wins with the Giants were the greatest, and I say no, which surprises them a little. I tell them the victory I liked most out of any I have ever had was when I was coaching the Giants and we went into Washington to play a very good Redskins team on a Monday night. To me, the Giants-Redskins games of that time were the greatest in the NFL. I loved to win in Washington because that was the toughest place to win, and for me, Joe Gibbs was the best coach I ever coached against. It was a great challenge. That year it looked like we were going to lose a heartbreaker, and we pulled it out on a long field goal on the last play of the game. All night long those sixty thousand Redskin fans were going crazy. In those situations, standing on the sidelines, you have to yell at one another to be heard. But as soon as the kick went through the goalposts, the stadium fell silent. The Redskins and all of their fans were stunned. We were running around, grabbing and hugging one another. We could have been whispering and heard every word. The most beautiful noise I have ever heard was the silence in the stadium that night.

It was the same way the next Saturday in Buffalo. We played a very tough defensive game, and hung on for the win. We beat New England to clinch a home playoff berth, and then beat Jacksonville in a playoff game to get to go to Denver for the AFC championship. It was an exhausting period of time for me. I just didn't have enough left to exercise every day, and when I start missing workouts it ruins me. With all the things on my mind, I was thinking about everything else but my health. I began to think 1998 was the end of the line.

Fortunately, I had a team I liked and in Leon Hess an owner who was supportive. I didn't have a lot of problems, and I didn't have a lot of jerks to deal with. There were only a handful of fines. The players were hungry and were willing to cooperate. They felt good about themselves. In 1997, when I first came to the Jets after they finished last in the league, we had a winning season, and that restored their dignity. I saw the transformation. They went from a group of guys who were beaten down to guys who were more confident. I saw the same thing in New England. I saw the same thing with the Giants. There's a distinct pattern, and when it happens, the team gets hungrier, wanting more challenges and victories.

I really started to see it happen in 1998 when we went into New England and beat them on a Monday night. Then we went to Kansas City and beat them at Arrowhead Stadium, where it's very difficult to win. They had won something like fifteen straight at home. We played them in the rain. It was a terrible day. But we made the plays and won the game. I could sense how our players felt right after the game: that they might actually do it. I told them afterward, "If you can go to a couple of more places like this, and do these things, you are going to be right in there at the end. This is what it takes."

We had what it took to beat Denver. We just didn't do it. I liked our attitude and our preparation going in. We were concerned about John Elway, but we thought we could handle him. I've played against John a few times over the years and felt we knew how to keep him from beating us. But their running back, Terrell Davis, is another story. He's one of the best I've ever seen, and I'm a guy who has made a study of great running backs. If I had my way, I'd run the ball every chance I had. That's my kind of game. Of course, you can't always do that, so you have to adjust what your game is to the kind of players you have on your squad. You can't really stop Terrell Davis. You just have to try to keep him from controlling the game, and we were doing that. If our team has the ball, they can't score points. We had the ball most of the first half, moving it pretty well, completing something like our first fifteen passes in a row. We had the lead at halftime, but it should have been bigger. We fumbled the ball a couple of times when we were in scoring position and made some other mistakes that came back to haunt us. Denver took the game away from us at the end.

It was hard to stand there and accept the loss. All we had to do was play solid football for another twenty-five minutes and we were in the Super Bowl. Most people don't realize what it took to get to that game. That's Mount Everest in my business. The plane ride home after a playoff loss is always the hardest.

You feel bad for your coaches, for your players, for your owner.

When we finally got home from Denver and landed in New York it had to be close to 2:00 in the morning. Mr. Hess was not able to make any road games because he'd been sick. Yet there he was. All dressed up and standing at the door of the plane, shaking hands, and saying a personal word to every person that got off the plane. I was really touched by that.

A few days after that a letter came to my office, from a friend of mine in the broadcast business. He nailed it pretty good. Here are a couple of lines from what he wrote:

> All those critical mistakes give birth to all those damn what-ifs. Hard to take I know. But, I also know that in time perspective will allow you to look back and smile at the things the club accomplished this year. Watching you speak after the game, I thought, it's not about a championship here or one there or catching lightning in a bottle for one season. It's a level of achievement accomplished year after year and not in a vacuum, but in a context in a particular set of realities. There are only a few of those who have ever coached the game that way, and you will be forever one of them.

The letter still gets to me. I keep it right here in my desk, and I've read it several times already. This guy understands. It's like being an old fighter. Every time you step out into the ring, you have to prove you still have it. That's my personality. That's what keeps me going. So I decided that I still wanted to climb into the ring, at least one more time, and prove I can compete. That I still had it. That I can still get to my team.

Above all, I returned in 1999 because of the feeling I have when we win. There's no feeling like it. But that feeling is what makes this an impossible job. No one can win all the time, and as good as the feeling is when you win, the feeling when you lose is ten times as bad. And the losing stays with you longer than the winning.

When I won my first Super Bowl back with the Giants in 1986, I wrote a book about my life. When I was with New England a few years back, I wrote a book about the comparisons between building a winning team and a winning business.

This book is about something I love: coaching football. This is going to be a week-to-week account of a coach's life. I want you to see how I worked with my coaching staff, prepared players, developed game strategies, and how we try to get it done over twenty-six weeks, twelve hours a day, without a day off from training camp through the end of the season.

An old friend of mine, Will McDonough, a sportswriter with the *Boston Globe*, who used to be on television with CBS and NBC, is going to help me on the project. Will and I have a great relationship. He knows more about me, and how I think, than just about anyone else. He'll get me to say some things I don't want to talk about. I only hope it's not too much.

APRIL 23, 1999

I just finished meeting with our draft choices and rookie free agents for the first time. The draft was last weekend, and it didn't have as much "juice" as usual because we did not have a first-round draft choice. We gave it to New England as part of the deal that brought me to the Jets three years ago.

After the draft was over, our scouts got on the phone right away and started signing free agents, the kids that did not get drafted but who we think still have a chance. I've brought them all in here for just the weekend as an orientation period. This is not a training camp per se. There are no veterans around, and I don't want them around because their presence can intimidate some of these kids. I don't want that to happen. Not just yet, anyway.

Today was a very important day for these kids and this organization. This is when we let them know what I feel pro football is about, and what they have to do to please me and win a job on this football team. We can sit a hundred people in the meeting room in our facility at Hofstra University on Long Island. We train at Hofstra all year long, so we don't need to go away to training camp like most teams do every July. Everything is done right here.

I set up this first meeting the same way every year. I stand at the podium on a small stage in front of the room. The players look up at me, trying to pay attention to what I'm telling them, but I know their minds are going in a million different directions.

For the most part, they don't quite know how to react. They're still trying to figure all of this out. For many of them, it's the first time they've ever been in New York or on a plane. My entire coaching and training staff sits right behind the players, and during the course of my speech I bring them up to the stage and introduce them one by one. This way the players have a chance to know what they look like and what each coach is responsible for.

I make a comment or two about each of the coaches. I tell the players to pay particular attention to who their position coach is and what they look like. Who the equipment man is, the trainer, and our weight coach. These are the people who they will be dealing with for most of the weekend. (Take a look at the appendix to get a complete breakdown of the coaching staff.)

I try not to overwhelm the kids, so I keep the speech simple, and I go over the same points several times, because this is the way you have to teach football players. A coach has to say things over and over again, and after a while, you can look into their eyes and see that the elevator is finally moving up a few floors. Some have elevators that move faster. Others might never get off the ground. This is the first time I have ever met these kids. I don't know how good they are. I've watched a lot of their college games on film, but mostly I relied on the opinions of my scouts and coaches.

Usually, you have a big name or two in the room. In New England, I had Drew Bledsoe, first pick in the entire draft, so everyone knew who he was. With the Giants and here with the Jets, every guy we picked on the first round had some kind of reputation. Without a first-round pick, and because we played so well last year and had one of the better records in the league, our first pick came in the second round, at number fifty-seven.

We took Randy Thomas, from Mississippi State, to fill our right guard position. We felt that he was the best guard in the country, and when he lasted to the fifty-seventh pick, we were rooting for him to still be there. Joey Clinkscales, our southeastern regional scout, picked him. He liked Thomas's athleticism and quickness. There was some question as to whether Thomas had good running ability, but we feel he has it.

One of the more important things we look for when we pick a player is that he is a worker, someone who will buy into our program. He has to be willing to lift weights and to condition himself. Besides the athletic ability, which has to be there, our experience has always been that the kids that are more self-starter-type guys are the ones who you eventually have more success with. The guys that you've got to kick all the time or push all the time, you sometimes fail with them because they get a little bit lazy. If a young player knows what he is going to have to do to play and recognizes opportunity when he sees it, he should be okay.

After the room settled down, I looked over the new players and the coaching staff and began talking.

Okay, fellas, I'm Bill Parcells. I'd like to welcome you to the New York Jets. This weekend is an orientation of sorts. This is a time where we try to get to know you guys and explain to you to the best of our ability how we do things and what we expect from you. To try to teach you in a short period of time the things we think will assist you in your efforts to make the team. In my experience, those people who accept these ideas succeed. Those that don't accept them usually have very little chance. It's in both our best interests that every one of you players succeed, so we're gonna try to be on the same page with you.

We're gonna explain things that, based on our experience, we feel are important in the pursuit of a professional football career. The competition level is going up, so some of those things are difficult. Now, before we go any further, I want to introduce our staff to give you a fix on those people you'll be dealing with here. I'm gonna start with four people who are in our support staff. So I'll ask Carl and David Price to come down to the front. Clay, are you here? Come on down front. And Steve Yarnell.

David Price, here in the brown shirt, is our head trainer. He talks to me and will talk to you about injuries. You don't talk to anyone else about injuries, including media members.

Clay Hampton is our head equipment man. Any equipment problems that you have or anything that you need, you go see Clay. Don't pick up anything in the locker room that does not belong to you. That is a good way to get out of here fast. If you need to have it, Clay knows where to get it. He's been doing this quite a while and will help you with what you need: type of shoes, the fitting of your helmet, shoulder pads, all of all that.

Carl Banks, a former NFL player, a real good one I might add, is in charge of our player development programs. He will help you adjust to the things outside of football, based on his experience and his knowledge of New York and the area—simple things such as how to set up a bank account, where to eat when you're on your own, where to do your laundry, where to go and where not to go—so you can survive in this community. Carl will help you look down the road at things like continuing education and internships. We want to make sure that our players have a chance to be successful both on the field and off the field. We started this program a couple of years ago, and we're doing well with it. A lot of our players are interning in the off-season with corporations and companies here in New York, and that helps them in the future.

The farthest on my right here is Steve Yarnell. He's our director of security and a former FBI agent. If you've got a problem that involves law enforcement, Steve's the man to go see. You can't be carrying guns around here, and he'll explain what the New York gun laws are. He can even help with an expired driver's license, things like that. Don't come into my office with your problems. Go to him and he'll speak with me.

We're not interested in players who have problems. We want you to put all the problems you have behind you. I don't need guys who have pregnant girlfriends that are calling them on the phone and all that shit. I am too old for it and I don't care about it. I want guys who can concentrate on being a football player.

Get focused and the next time we see you, which will be in the middle of May, the last cuts in training camp, then you have a chance. So put the problems away.

I'm gonna introduce the coaches to you. Try to fix on your position coach to know what's going on here. First up is our quarterback coach Dan Henning, next to Dan is our tight end coach Pat Hodgson, right here is our running back coach Mo Carthon, Bill Belichick is our defensive coordinator and coaches the secondary. Eric Mangini is our defensive quality control coach and helps with the secondary, majoring with the safeties. Romeo Crennel has been with me the longest, over twenty years. He's our defensive line coach. Bill Muir is our offensive line coach, Al Groh is our linebacker coach, Charlie Weis is our offensive coordinator, and he also coaches what we call the x-position, which is a combination of the fullback and tight end position. John Lott is our strength coach. You'll be spending the most time with him on your first introduction to the Jets.

I'm gonna call these names in alphabetical order. This is my first time seeing some of you, so when I call your name I want you to stand up, repeat your name if I pronounced it incorrectly, tell us what school you're from and what position you play. We're gonna start with James Adderly, Ed Conti, Shawn Foreman, Dirk Johnson, Jermaine Jones, Courtney Ledyard, Del Lee, Greg Lotysz, David Loverne, J. P. Machado, Marc Megna, Jason Mills, Jason Poles, J. J. Syvrud, Randy Thomas, Jermaine Wiggins, Jason Wiltz, Ryan Young. Did I miss anybody?

Okay, guys. Let me tell you a little bit about the purpose of this camp, what we're trying to do here. We are trying to introduce you to, like I said, the way we do things. We'll give you a few fundamental drills. We're going to give you a little introduction to the football, but you'll get more of that when you come back here in late May, early June.

Now let's talk about the weight program. The veteran players you're gonna be competing with have been here for two and a half hours a day, four days a week for the last five weeks.

They've got twenty workouts in, and they're headed for forty workouts prior to their minicamp the last week of May. Those guys are here.

Also, our running program this week was five 350-yard strides on Monday. Ten 160's on Tuesday. And sixteen 110's on Wednesday.

That should give you an idea of our conditioning program and what we're gonna expect. When you come back for training camp, we have a conditioning test. If you don't pass the test, you're probably not gonna be here very long. It's important to me as the head coach. I want well-conditioned players at the proper weight with good stamina and endurance. That's what I'm looking for. Everything you do from here on out is evaluated. Don't try to be inconspicuous because we're gonna look for you. Everything you do is part of the evaluation process. We base our evaluations on a few things.

First of all, we don't feel responsible as a coaching staff to come to the hotel and wake you up to make sure you're where you're supposed to be. You just need to be there. And you need to be on time. You don't walk into these meetings a minute late. In pro football, if you're late you get fined. And it's a lot of money. If you oversleep we'll begin to feel that you're not dependable and we can't count on you. Maybe you're always in trouble, you've got girl problems, or you drink too much, or you use drugs. Any kind of problem that detracts from your ability to help our team perform lessens your chances of being around here. I have zero tolerance for that stuff, so get the message.

My coaches and I, all we do is coach. We don't go out, and we don't recruit, or talk to alumni groups like your college coaches did. We don't do anything but coach professional football. We are here to win games. We try to win every game that we play, beginning in the preseason and through the regular season, and if we're in the tournament. We've got a pretty good team here. It's not great, but it's pretty good. There's a high competition level, so if you want to be successful, you're gonna have to compete on that level.

Now don't come in here and say, "Bill, you owe me a chance." I don't owe you anything. You make your own chances. One of the most important things we evaluate you on is whether you know what to do on a given play. I always use this example every year. Odell, you're a running back, right? If Odell Collins does not know his first assignment—the blitz pickup rules—I am not going to play him in the preseason games, understand? You are not even getting into the game.

Why not? You are going to get my quarterback knocked out for the season. Then I am going to have a team rebellion on my hands because we do not have a first-team quarterback. So if you do not know who to block on the blitz, you're not playing, you're not even going near the field. And that goes for some of the rest of you. If you do not know what to do, you're not going to play.

You need to study. If you do not know, you do not sit there and pretend you do. You need to go to your position coach and find out exactly how we want you to do things. If it is still not clear and everybody else around you seems to look like they understand it and you do not, and you are afraid to raise your hand or afraid to talk to them, that is stupidity on your part. If you don't find out what to do you're not going to play. It is their job to teach you, but it is your job to find out.

Execution is also important. Now, gentlemen, if our receivers coach, Todd Haley, tells you to run a fifteen-yard comeback but you run a twelve, and you are open before we are ready to throw it, he will correct you. Then let's say you run eighteen and you are still not precise. If you don't have a good feel of what to do or are unable to make a judgment that allows you to do it, you are not going to play. Do what we tell you, not what is instinctive to you.

The next thing is, can you be the same person every day? Do I see some of you guys come out to practice and one day you look like a world-beater, the next day you're just a little too tired and just can't keep up?

Training camp is hard. You have to have some staying power.

You will hear me say that a lot. You are young players. You don't know what to expect. You don't know where the camp is going. You don't know anything about the competition. You don't know anything about anything. You are just out there trying to do it, and those of you that have got the drive to hang in there and execute the way we need, we will start noticing.

Item number four: stamina. For example, Adderly, if you can only run your routes when you feel good or early in practice when you still have your quickness, but you're not in good enough condition to run them later, we will work you. We will run you more than you've ever run before. You'll run more patterns, more drills, and more routes. We're only going to have three deep at a position, maybe four at the most, so we need guys who can endure.

The last thing is talent. The first four things should be equal for everybody in this room. Everybody should know what to do, everybody should try to follow their assignments, everybody should be reliable and dependable and consistent, and everybody should be in condition.

Then it comes down to what kind of talent you have. If you have enough talent to play, but there's not enough roster spots here or you just don't fit in, somebody is going to see it. Someone will see it, and you will wind up with a job somewhere else. How do you get on the team? Here is what most of you are thinking: "Let's see, I'm a wide receiver, I guess they are going to keep me. They will probably keep four or five or maybe six wide receivers. They're going to keep maybe two or three tight ends, and maybe four or five backs, and maybe eight or nine offensive linemen, maybe ten." That is what some of you are thinking. That is the wrong way to think.

You're in competition not only with that fourth wide receiver, or that fifth wide receiver, or seventh linebacker. You are also in competition with all the other linebackers on other teams that might be cut. We have scouts out all summer looking at other teams for a reason. You're also in competition with other position players: the tight ends and safeties and wide receivers for the last spot on this team. During the season I meet with my coaches three nights a week to discuss who we take to the game to allow them to have enough practice time. There is a fifty-three-man roster. We are allowed to take forty-five plus a third quarterback, forty-six players. That means seven players stay home.

It always comes down to the forty-first, forty-second, forty-third, and forty-fourth guys. Who are they? They're guys that when we put them in the game, we know that we're gonna get x number of plays out of them. So, I happen to know Foreman. You played defense for a while, didn't you? Now he's a wide receiver who has played defense. That makes me think that he might be able to tackle somebody. If he can tackle somebody, he might be more valuable to me than a better wide receiver who can't tackle anybody. Maybe I can use him on punt returns. Maybe he's tough enough to cover kickoffs. I don't know, but if he is, he has a better chance versus somebody who can't do that. The question you need to ask yourself is, "How do I get to the game?" Now, you say I'm not covering kickoffs. But, you know what, you might be in the wedge covering kickoff returns. You might be a good punt return holdup guy. Linebackers, especially, have got to do it all; you've got to be on all those special teams or you're not going to the game. I have a defensive player named Bobby Hamilton here that plays an average of fifteen, sixteen plays on special teams a week. When I take Bobby Hamilton to games, he's not a starter. He'll play a little bit on defense and fifteen or sixteen plays on special teams. Altogether that's about twenty plays. I know he's going to contribute, and that's valuable to a coach, as opposed to somebody who's standing on the sideline not doing anything.

There are positions available on offense, defense, and special teams. These positions are highly competitive. The more positions you can fill and do them well, the better chance you have to compete. If you have a particular skill—say you're a snapper. Now, I don't need guys that are trying to be a snapper who have never snapped in their lives. But if you snap, step up and let our special teams coach, Mike Sweatman, know. If you're a punt returner, I mean a legitimate punt returner—I don't feel like manufacturing punt returners—if you've got some confidence there, let Coach Sweatman know. If you've played any position on the punt team or kickoff team, let him know. He'll check to see if you can do some of those things. So that's another way to get onto the team. You've got your position as well as your special teams position.

There's a lot of competition coming from everywhere for the last spot. It's from your own group, from within other groups on your team, it's players on other teams who might do it better than you do. That's the way it is, that's the way it will always be until you leave the league.

What we're gonna do from here on out is something like this: the NCAA has rules that prohibit players from coming to their pro team before they finish their schoolwork. We've checked on all your schools and there are two players here, Conti and Loverne, whose school's final exams finish after May 16. We're gonna bring you guys back in here about May 16. We'll take care of you. We're gonna have a place for you to sleep at Hofstra, you don't have to pay for that. We're gonna give you seventy dollars a day for food. That's about four hundred dollars a week for food. You need some type of transportation, because we're not gonna be driving you around. In the first ten days when you come back, we're gonna put you in our off-season program with John Lott. Then we're gonna have a veteran mini-camp. I usually never put the rookies in with the vets, but this time I'm gonna put you guys in with the vets. Then I'm gonna keep some vets and all you guys in the first week of June and I'm gonna give you another workout. When the coaches go on vacation, the rookies will stay here until July.

There's a day absence, when the draft choices have to go to a rookie symposium in northern Virginia. Carl Banks will take you. The rest of you will stay here and train with John. When you leave here on July 9, you'll be in the condition to make that your position. You'll be stronger, you'll be ready to compete at the best level that you can. At the veteran minicamp you'll see how a pro ball team operates. You'll get a good opportunity. We're gonna do everything we can to help you succeed.

Now let me tell you this. Everyone on this team is going to have a reporting weight. We're gonna test some of you to see if you can lose some weight. Just to see if you've got enough discipline to do it and train and get in shape and run and lose a few pounds. If you don't lose the weight and you come in overweight, it's $93 per pound, per day. So some of you fat guys if you're ten pounds over, that's $930 a day, and the next week if you're nine pounds over then it's nine times $93. Now we're not just gonna indiscriminately say to the big guys who are 320 pounds to get down to 280. We're not stupid. We're gonna take a look at you and do some body fat testing. We'll see what kind of stamina you've got, whether you can do anything at all. John and I will talk and try to give you a reporting weight that's good and gives you the best chance to succeed.

Other than that, fellas, I want you to be on time. I want you to pay attention when you're here and I want you to help us win games. Some guys get onto pro football teams and they start walking around thinking they're important because they play for the New York Jets. I don't like guys that think they're important. I don't like guys hanging out in the bars with New York Jets shit on, walking around like you did something. You haven't done anything yet. Stay out of the bar in the hotel. It's off limits. I don't want any party guys. Don't touch anything in the locker room that doesn't belong to you. We have some stuff—T-shirts, hats, and duffel bags. We'll have all that to give you when you leave for home.

Next thing, tomorrow will be your first exposure to the media. I don't want to hear anything about how you're going to do, about how great you are, or who you're gonna beat out. All of you are just trying to make a contribution to the team. You're gonna do the best you can. You're gonna try to get an understanding of what it takes to play pro football. You're rookie players. Act like rookie players. There's no shame in that. Everyone on this team was a rookie once. Be humble. The New York press is very difficult and I'm gonna say this a couple of times: don't think they're trying to be friends with you. Some guy comes up to you and all of a sudden he's your new best friend. Just be very businesslike, be honest, be cordial, be receptive, give him a direct answer, but don't try to be friends with him, because they don't care about friendship. They're just trying to get in. That's their job. You never know who you're talking to in New York. Be suspicious.

My dad used to tell me something that served me very well. I tell my team this all the time. Don't go anyplace around here where you're not known or you're not welcome and you'll stay out of trouble.

Now, what we're gonna do is have offensive and defensive meetings here. The defensive players are gonna go with Coach Belichick down the hall. And the offensive players will go with Coach Weis. We're gonna have you here until about nine o'clock tonight. Now here's the deal, [Randy] Thomas. You're in charge of the vans. You got me? Since you're the highest draft choice we've got, that means you're responsible for making sure that everybody's ass is on the van before it comes over here at eight-thirty. If somebody is not on the van, I'm holding you responsible, so you figure out how to do it. We'll have a meeting in the morning. We'll have breakfast, then we'll come back here for a meeting.

We're gonna have indoor testing tomorrow morning: bench press, vertical jumps, and the standing broad jump. We will also be testing for flexibility and stretching. We'll have outdoor testing in the afternoon: forty-yard dashes, backpedaling, and agility drills, that kind of thing.

Then we'll explain a little bit about May 16. What we're gonna do, how we're gonna get you in here, and all that kind of stuff.

We're gonna have a weight program presentation. Pay attention to that. If you're not doing cleans and squats, you're gonna have a hard time here. They are the staple exercises of the New

York Jets. Anybody know how to do a clean? We'll see about that. Any questions now, fellas? Ask them now. Like I said, don't be stupid if you misunderstand something.

We're trying to win championships here, fellas. That's what we're here to do. We're not here to look good. We're not playing for second place. We play to win. My players have that mentality now. You have to get that mentality that is gonna allow you to be successful. We're here to help you. That's what we're gonna do from here on out.

If you're sensitive, you're gonna have a hard time around here. I have a bad temper. I swear, I yell, I do a lot of things. If you're sensitive, you're gonna have a hard time. If you're not sensitive, you'll get along fine. I'm not asking you to be a tin soldier. Just be who you are, but pay attention, be on time, be in shape, and try to help us win games.

See you in the morning.

Offense, you're going with Coach Weis. Defense, you're going with Coach Belichick.

That was the speech. Now these guys are going to hear shorter versions of the same speech over and over again, as long as they play for me. There's nothing that kills a coach more, or blows a game for him faster, than someone who doesn't know what he is supposed to do on any given play.

Let me give you a few examples so you understand.

I was coaching New England in the Super Bowl against Green Bay. Before the game we told Willie Clay, one of our safeties who made the calls and changes in the defensive backfield, what to do in certain situations against the Packer offense. Now, Willie is a smart player, that's why we gave him the job of trying to get the people around him in the right places. One of the things we told Willie is when Brett Favre checks off and calls an audible at the line of scrimmage, we automatically get out of what we have on. Favre must see something he likes and is ready to attack our defense, and we don't want to give it to him.

On the Packers' second play of the game, Favre checked off.

We're in man-to-man coverage. Clay was supposed to change our defense and get us into a three-deep zone. But it didn't happen. We got caught in man-to-man, and Favre beat us down the middle of the field with a long touchdown pass to Andre Rison. Our cornerback on the play covering Rison, Otis Smith, took the heat from the media. But it really wasn't his fault. Otis, who is now with me here at the Jets, had the outside or sideline responsibility. He thought he had help in the middle of the field from Lawyer Milloy, a rookie safety for us that year. Clay never made the call. If he had, Milloy, instead of covering the tight end man-to-man in the flat, would have dropped in the middle of the field, and we would have had the play covered. When we asked Willie later why he didn't do it, he said he knew what to do, but he just couldn't get it out of his throat. So we were behind, 7–0, in a hurry.

Later in the game, we had a defense on where Milloy lined up man-to-man on the line of scrimmage against Antonio Freeman. Freeman has great speed. We knew Milloy couldn't run with him. Milloy knew he couldn't run with Freeman. So we told Milloy before the game, "If we get in this situation, and we can't get out of it, you hit him hard right at the line of scrimmage. Jam him, slow him down, so his speed won't be that big a factor." But just before the ball was snapped Milloy started to back off. He didn't get a good piece of Freeman, who ran past him to catch another long touchdown bomb. Two errors because guys didn't do what they were supposed to do. Two touchdowns.

Last year here with the Jets we were in a playoff game against Jacksonville. We were doing a very good job against them defensively. Their offense couldn't get much going, and we had a comfortable lead with just a few seconds left in the half. We called a prevent defense, where the number one rule is that our free safety, Jerome Henderson, doesn't let anyone get behind him, no matter what.

With just a couple of seconds left in the half, Jacksonville, with time for just one play, was too far away to try a field goal, so you know they are going to try to throw the ball into the end zone. They did, and scored a touchdown. Henderson let the guy get behind him. A mortal sin in that defense. But he did. And he gave Jacksonville some life going into the locker room. Fortunately, we made enough plays in the second half to keep the lead and win the game.

The year before, on the final game of the season in Detroit when we needed a win to get into the playoffs, we had two beauties. But I had to shoulder the blame for some of what happened. I was just too aggressive that game and probably overcoached it to some degree.

We were doing a great job against Barry Sanders. He was going for two thousand yards that day, and we shut him down pretty good for three quarters. We had the lead in the fourth period and were driving for a score that should have put the game away for us. On first down, I called a halfback option pass to be thrown by a rookie, Leon Johnson. Now this kid is a very talented all-round athlete. Our coaching staff, in looking at the Detroit defense on film during the week, felt we could score in close with the halfback option. We practiced it all week. But we told Johnson, if the receiver is not wide open, throw the ball away. Don't risk an interception. The receiver was covered, he threw an interception. They came back and beat us.

Coaches remember those plays even more than they do touchdowns. They haunt us. As coaches, we are not supposed to let this happen. And sometimes you fall into the trap of giving a player, especially a young player, too much too soon, to a point where he is overcoached. With most guys, you have to spoon-feed them a little at a time and in a sequence that makes sense. If you tell him everything you know, or everything you think he needs to know, he can become confused. You can't give him too many things to think about. If you do, when he goes out on the field he's not just playing football. He's not reacting naturally to what is going on. Instead, before the ball is snapped he's thinking about what he's supposed to do. And if he's thinking about twenty things at once, chances are he is not going to function too well.

• • •

My first coaching job was in Hastings, Nebraska, just after I finished playing linebacker at Wichita State. I was coaching for a
guy named Dean Pryor, and during the season we were coming
up for a big game against Nebraska Wesleyan. Our best player
was a fullback named Jack Giddings. Good player, great kid.
Worked hard. Did anything you wanted him to do. I was
twenty-three years old at the time, coaching my ass off, or so I
thought.

Wesleyan had been scoring a lot of points all year, and their
big play was a bootleg option. They scored at least one touchdown in every game on it. I knew they were not going to score
on us. In those days, players had to play both ways. Offense and
defense. Giddings was our fullback on offense, and our safety on
defense. All week long, I pounded it into him how we were not
going to let them have this bootleg, and how we were going to
stop it. We spent all kinds of time, maybe too much, defending
this play. Well, the game came, Wesleyan got close to the goal
line and ran the play. The quarterback faked a bootleg outside,
and threw a pass for a touchdown. I went crazy on the sideline.
I wanted to kill Giddings. He came to the sideline and I got in his
face, ripping him up and down. Then I heard the voice of Dean
Pryor telling me to knock it off and shut up.

I said, "But, Coach, I worked on this all week and there's no
way this should have happened!" And then Pryor said something that I took from that moment with me the rest of my
coaching career. He said, "You obviously didn't coach it well
enough." And he was right. The coach shares the responsibility
with the player. No matter how hard we work on something, or
prepare the player to do it, if he doesn't get it done for us, then
we have to share some of the blame. Then we need to figure
out how both of us, player and coach, can get it done right the
next time. Time and trouble have taught me that there is a fine
line between what a player can handle under pressure and
what he can't.

THE DEATH OF LEON HESS

We buried Mr. Hess this morning, and I miss him already. I loved the guy and I had tremendous respect for him. To me, he was what an owner should be—he was in it to win. He wanted a team he could be proud of. When I first took the job he told me he was tired of being embarrassed by his team. I didn't ever want him to feel that way again as long as I coached for him. I know he got a kick out of the two years we had together, and they will always be special in my memory.

We talked a lot on the phone. He'd call me a couple of times a week at about eight in the morning to discuss the team, see how things were going, and to make sure everything was okay. We also talked about Jersey.

When I was a kid, growing up in Hackensack, my father used to take me down to the river, and we'd sit there and watch these pontoon planes land. Mr. Hess had some oil tanks across the Hackensack River in a town called Richfield Park. My dad was director of industrial relations for U.S. Rubber, which has since become Uniroyal. Like Mr. Hess he worked in New York City, right in the middle of Manhattan, at Sixth Avenue and Forty-ninth Street, and was from Jersey, so he knew a lot about him. He told me stories about how Mr. Hess grew up down the road in Asbury Park, digging clams as a kid and selling them. Then taking that money and buying his first truck. Then he had six trucks. And then he built an oil refinery, and eventually Hess Oil.

*Leon Hess supported me every step of the way. No coach could ask for a
better owner.*

Mr. Hess was a quiet man, but he had a great sense of humor. I think the reason we hit it off so well was that we thought a lot alike. He was something like twenty-five years older than me, but we came from the same environment. Growing up in New Jersey you see both sides. You are confronted with the good and the bad. You deal with some rough-and-tumble people on occasion. And you are growing up in a melting pot of different ethnic cultures with mostly blue-collar people who work hard. You have got to make choices. Mr. Hess, who never had more than a high school education, went on to become one of the most successful men in the world. His life is a tremendous story. He was also a very generous and giving man. He donated freely to charities and was truly loved by the people who were close to him. People had the greatest admiration for the type of person he was.

I really didn't know him that well until I took this job. I met him a couple of times at league meetings when I was with the Giants. I think Wellington Mara introduced us. But I respected him from a distance. By being in New York all of those years I saw how hard he tried to do the right thing. As an owner he was a traditional guy and wanted to do what was right for the league. He didn't come into this thing to make money. He loved the game, like the Maras, the Rooneys, the Ralph Wilsons, the guys who made the game great and still do. He wasn't in it to jump in front of TV cameras and become a celebrity. The only time he spoke directly to the team was on Thanksgiving each year. Last Thanksgiving he came to practice, and when he gave me the signal, I called the players into a circle, and Mr. Hess spoke for just a few minutes. He told the players he wished them success, how he thought things were going well and that we could make the playoffs, and he liked the way they were behaving as a team. His speech didn't take more than a handful of minutes, yet every player and coach realized that they had his support 100 percent.

The first time I ever spoke to him about coaching the Jets he was, as he would always be, straight and to the point. It was after I left the Patriots, when we had just been to the Super Bowl. We had to go through a lot of bullshit for it to happen, but he just wanted me to coach for him and didn't care what it took. The first time we talked was on the telephone.

A lot of people have theories about what happened before this conversation, but none of them know what they're talking about. I never had any contact with Mr. Hess or anyone from the Jets until after I left the Patriots. And my agent, Robert Fraley, didn't either. Now, I'll tell you who started the ball rolling. My sister-in-law, Elaine, who is married to my brother Don. Elaine worked as a secretary for a good friend of Mr. Hess, and one day he said to her that Mr. Hess was upset with the Jets coaching staff and was going to make a change. She told him, "Well, tell him to get my brother-in-law, Bill Parcells." She planted the seed. At the time I had an option year left on my contract, which had to be exercised by both parties to go into effect. I decided I didn't want to coach there anymore. There's still a mistaken belief that I had another year left on my contract. That's incorrect.

Anyway, Mr. Hess was in his office with Steve Gutman, the team president, and my agent, Robert Fraley. I was home in New Jersey. Mr. Hess said, "How does this sound?" He told me I could coach just as long as I wanted to. One year. Two years. Three. Then be general manager if that is what I wanted. Truth is, I didn't want to coach anywhere but New York. I was very comfortable in New England, but it was time for me to go home.

Of course, it wasn't so simple. New England had protested my going to the Jets, even though in my mind my contract with them was over. The commissioner didn't see it that way, so Mr. Hess was trying to work out a settlement. In the interim, he was going to hire Bill Belichick as head coach.

Steve Gutman came up with the Belichick plan. It was clever. If things didn't work out, Bill Belichick would be head coach for a season. If, on the other hand, I was able to join the Jets, then I would become head coach and Belichick would again become my assistant. The agreement also said that if I left as head coach, he was going to be the next guy. They gave him a nice deal—he became the highest paid assistant coach in the history of the NFL.

Now Mr. Hess didn't tell me at the time what the settlement with New England was going to be, and when he did, I told him not to do it and to just go with Gutman's plan. But Mr. Hess said he would deal with it, and he did. When I told him the price—a handful of draft picks, including a first rounder—was too steep, he said he didn't care. He was old. He wanted to win. And he didn't want to wait. I told him he was making a mistake. He told me it didn't matter what I thought, he was doing it. So that was it.

From the day I signed on until he passed away, we never had a single conversation where he was not positive, or did not encourage me. He was at his best in the worst of times. My first year we lost a terrible game to the Colts at home. I felt before the game that if we won, we would win the division and be in the playoffs for sure. Our chances looked good: we had beaten them earlier in the year in Indianapolis. But we played lousy, and they beat us bad, 22–14. That was my lowest point with the Jets. In the dressing room after the game, I apologized to Mr. Hess for the way we played. And when I did, he looked me right in the eye and said, "You know, we've got a better football team around here than we used to have and I can tell because I've watched all of them play. You just keep doing what you are doing, and don't worry about it." He stood so tall even after a tough loss.

When we flew into New York after losing the AFC championship game to Denver, he was right at the plane, waiting. At one in the morning, in the freezing cold. And he knew he was dying and didn't have a lot of time. But he felt so bad he couldn't make the trip. I was the first one off the plane and he shook my hand, said nice going, and that we just came up a little bit short. Then he stood there shaking the hand of every coach, every player, every equipment guy, and saying a word to each and every one of them.

I'll always keep that memory of him, with one other. The way he was in the locker room after we beat Jacksonville in the playoffs the week before. It might not be the right word, but "giddy" is the way I would describe him. He was so happy. The joy on his face was like that of a little kid. It meant so much to him. To win at home. To make those loyal Jet fans happy. He lived for that moment. I know he did.

The last conversation I ever had with him probably tells as much about the man as any experience we shared. When the '98 season was over, I knew we had to get some more players if we wanted to get to the Super Bowl. We didn't have much of a draft, because we were still paying off draft choices to New England for the deal Mr. Hess made to bring me here.

So I had to get better through free agency, and make sure we wrapped up some of our own top players. We had to come up with a lot of cash to pay some bonuses. We gave Vinny Testaverde a new deal that gave him $11 million guaranteed on a $16 million contract. Then I picked up Tom Tupa, a punter I had in New England who can also play quarterback. We gave him $1.6 million. Then tight end Eric Green got $1.8 million. At that point, I wasn't actively looking for any more players. We had just about spent all of the money we had. Then Roman Phifer of the Rams became available. I thought, dammit, this kid is a good football player. He can help us. I'm going to give it a shot. I called and told him I knew Detroit had an interest, but that I wanted to speak with him about coming to the Jets. He came in and we wound up signing the guy. Next thing I knew, Steve Gutman was in my office. He had this very concerned look on his face. He says to me, "Bill, this has to stop. Are we trying to win at all costs?"

I said, "Yup. That's what we are trying to do."

"Do you mean at all costs?"

"Yup, that's what I pretty much mean, Steve."

I told him to rest easy because I didn't have any more money to spend under the salary cap. There was nothing left. I told him I had a chance to get a good football player and that's why I did it.

After our conversation, I started to think maybe I was going a little bit overboard here. So I decided to give Mr. Hess a call. I never called him in the afternoon, so he must have thought it was important because he took the call.

"Leon," I said, "this is Bill. You know I don't have much of a draft this year because you gave away all of the choices, and the only way I can improve the team is with free agents and spending money for the players." And then I went on and told him not to worry because I wasn't going to spend any more money.

Know what he said to me?

"Bill, I don't give a shit. As a matter of fact, if you need some more money, just come on over here and we will borrow some from the oil company. I'll have it this afternoon."

Isn't that something? Then he said: "Kid, you're doing a great job. Just keep it up."

I cried when he died. It was just after five in the morning when Steve Gutman called and told me he had passed away during the night. I knew it was coming. I knew it was close. And yet I cried. I felt sorry for his suffering, but I also selfishly felt sorry for myself. I cried again at his services when one of his granddaughters eulogized him. When the young woman spoke from her heart about how he was always there for his family and friends, how he was a very kind, understanding, and generous man, it really hit home with me.

The man's word was his bond. You could count on him coming through, even if something was said in some vague conversation. If it was said, that was good enough for him. When we first talked about me coming to coach the Jets, I told him we were the only team on the East Coast that didn't have a practice bubble for cold weather. He said don't worry, you'll have it when you need it, and sure enough, we did.

When the memorial service for Mr. Hess was over, I told Wellington Mara I wanted him to take special care of himself, because now, with Mr. Hess gone, there weren't many of the old great ones left. Every time this league loses one of the old guard, it loses another piece of its heart.

JULY 5, 1999

In this job, you can take your body on vacation but never your mind. You can't shut that off. I'm reading the paper this morning and I see that the new owner of the Washington Redskins, Daniel Snyder, has fired twenty-five people in the organization. He doesn't even own the team for a month and he gets rid of twenty-five people.

This is when I ask myself if the next one in here is going to be another Daniel Snyder. If he is, I'm gone. I don't need any owner-operators in my life anymore. I hope that is not going to be the case. A few days after Mr. Hess died, his son John had a meeting with me to explain how the process for the sale of the team was going to work. John told me that he was aware of all the things in my contract with the Jets, that I can coach as long as I want, and then when I decide to stop coaching, turn it over to Bill Belichick. John and three other people designated by his father were going to carry out Leon Hess's wishes.

Mr. Hess put it right in his will that he wanted the team sold and that he no longer wanted his family involved. I think he saw some of the problems other owners in the league before him had with their children fighting over the team after they were gone. He didn't want that to happen. They hired Goldman Sachs here in New York City to find potential buyers. Then, with the help of Steve Gutman and the trustees of Mr. Hess's estate, they'll select the next owner. I hope the process will be smooth, but I'd rather not have it finalized until this season is over. I don't want some new owner jumping in and making changes while we're trying to win some games. I think this team is in pretty good shape to take a run at this thing, so I don't need any unnecessary problems.

Now, I've been through a couple of these owner situations. Like someone coming in to buy any company, they are going to have a different way of doing things than the previous owner. He can do what he likes, but if he tries to do something that's a material breach of my contract, then he's going to have to pay me off and get me out of here. Then he would have to get new leadership people, but if that's what he wants to do, fine with me.

Some friends of mine, when I talk about this possibility, tell me no way any new owner would fire me. Really. Well, Jerry Jones fired Tom Landry in a heartbeat and Tom was one of the greatest coaches the game has ever seen. Paul Brown had the team named after himself, had played in ten straight championship games, and Art Modell owned the team for three years and fired him. Wayne Huizenga had the Dolphins for what, two or three years, and Don Shula, who won more games than any coach in pro football history, was gone.

What I'm saying is, it doesn't make a bit of difference what has happened in the past. If the new owner wants to run it all himself, that's fine with me. He buys it, it belongs to him. He can run it any way he likes. By the same token, if he wants what we had done here perpetuated, that's fine with me as well.

For the most part, I've been lucky with owners. Two out of three is pretty good. Of course, I was spoiled the last two years with Mr. Hess. As far as I'm concerned, he was the perfect owner. In the last chapter I talked about how he desperately wanted to win and would spend to win. A very private and very secure man, he wasn't interested in using the team to become a celebrity.

The owners during my first head coaching job with the Giants, Wellington and Tim Mara, were good people and fine owners. They didn't get along with each other, but they had one common interest. They wanted the Giants to win. Both of them treated me well. Because they were at odds with each other, we had a unique situation with the Giants. George Young, our general manager, served as a buffer between them and did a great job handling that situation as well as keeping any problems the Maras might have had away from me and the football operation. Never once did anything that Wellington did, or Tim did, affect me as a coach. We did things as a group. Even with personnel, or in the draft, most of the time we were on the same page. I'll admit I didn't have a great relationship with Tom Boisture, who was in charge of personnel when I was with the Giants. Let me explain.

What most people don't understand, even the biggest pro football fan, is that there is a natural animosity between coaches and scouts. It's difficult for the two to get along because when the scout says, "This guy has ability," the coach can say, "Yeah, he's got ability but he's just not doing it." That's when you get the conflict. Still Tom and I didn't have many problems, and none that ever hurt. Never did the Giants try to push any players on me. They knew the kind of players I wanted and they tried to get them. I was lucky with them.

I left the Giants because of heart trouble. I joined NBC for two years and had some fun as an analyst and commentator. But it wasn't like being in the action. During my second year on television, after my heart bypass, I knew I wanted to be back. I went out to do a game, and being in the stadium got me going. When the year was over I was ready to return to coaching.

Someone told me that New England was interested in me, but at that time I had no assurance that was the case. I interviewed with James B. Orthwein and some of his advisors. I liked what they said about giving me more control than I had with the Giants. I was going to be the guy they wanted to go in and reorganize the franchise and get the team back on its feet again. The Patriots had the worst record the year before. At the time, it was a job, but not a very good chance. But it gave me a challenge I wanted. I knew I could coach. I wanted to find out if I could be a general manager. So I took the job.

Orthwein was from St. Louis and he wanted to pull the team out of New England and get it to St. Louis, or failing that, sell it for the highest price. He told me when he hired me he considered me as an asset, as part of a potential sale. That's why he gave me a five-year contract. It had an unusual stipulation: if I left during those five years, I had to pay him back $1 million. He figured that money would force me to stay around with the new owner, even if I didn't like him.

The problem with coaching for Orthwein was that he didn't want to spend any money. Take the worst team in the league at the time, and turn it around, but don't go over budget. My first year, we had the second lowest payroll in the league. I think only Cincinnati spent less than we did, and this was before the salary cap. As a result, we couldn't compete the first couple of seasons in free agency, and this hurt us later as a team. I had to sign anyone I could get that was better than what we had. And we didn't have much, but some of the guys we brought in were still better, even though they might not have looked it. I called those guys "hold the fort" players. These are guys you bring in to fill holes until you can find someone better. We did the same thing my first year with the Jets.

Aside from recognizing me as an asset, Orthwein didn't really know who I was when he hired me. And he had no particular interest in trying to improve the team. Once I got there, it was apparent to me that they wanted my name to help sell tickets, and that they really didn't have any concern about trying to win games or improve the franchise. They wanted to enhance the value of the franchise simply by putting a stronger personality in to run it.

The best player on the team at the time was a guy named Irving Fryar. It was time to redo his contract, and they didn't want to hear about it. So rather than lose him the next year to free agency and get nothing for him, I traded him for a couple of draft choices. I knew we weren't going to be any good that first year anyway, but we would have been a better team with

Fryar, who had great years with Miami and Philadelphia after he left us.

In all my years with the Giants, I think there was only one change in the business end of the operation, and that was someone leaving to get married. After Bob Kraft bought the team from Orthwein, we had more than twenty people leave in three years. Everyone has a different style. But I also understood, and still do, that the owner has the right to do anything he wants. It's his team, and if he wants to make changes, good luck to him. But I don't have to be a part of it if I don't want to, and that is what happened in New England with Kraft, even though we had great success on the field in the three years we were together.

Kraft did a lot of good things in New England. He and his sons did a tremendous job marketing the team and generating more revenue. More importantly for me, they brought stability to the franchise and were committed to putting a good team on the field, keeping the team in New England, and improving the stadium. Kraft let us spend the money Orthwein wouldn't spend. If Orthwein let me re-sign some veteran players I had at the time—Bruce Armstrong, Ben Coates, Fryar, Maurice Hurst—we would have had so much more money available under the salary cap. The second year we could have been more competitive, and that was the year we went to the playoffs. But we were forced to wait until Kraft came in with some fresh money. We did improve what we did in free agency, and the first year we had a helluva draft with Drew Bledsoe, Chris Slade, Todd Rucci, Vincent Brisby, and Troy Brown. As of this date, all of those guys are still there and are productive.

As far as the football operation was concerned, the first year Kraft was pretty much hands off. Like I said, with the twenty people leaving he made a lot of administrative changes, and quite frankly, a lot of them needed to be made. But even in the first year, I could see that Kraft wanted to get his hands on the team and be the person deciding what was going to happen. He wanted to become an owner/operator. I thought I was the operator. That was my deal when I came to the team. That's when I decided to move on.

When I came to the Jets I didn't know if Mr. Hess was an owner or an operator. He turned out to be an owner, and a great one. Owners can work well with coaches. Operators are hard to work with. They've got their own ideas.

Now, I'm wondering what the next Jets owner is going to be like. No matter what, I know it's going to be different. The other day I was asked if I "feared" what the next owner might bring. I answered that I was too old to be fearful. I know there is not going to be anyone here like Leon Hess. It's not going to run like it did the last couple of years when he was here. There are all different kinds of motives when a person wants to buy a team. I hope I get someone I can communicate with, someone who really wants to win and is committed to winning.

My experiences in New England prepared me a little bit for where I am right now. With the Patriots, there were stories almost every day about the team moving or being sold. Right now with the Jets, there is a lot of paranoia. It's a natural reaction. All the employees in our building are concerned. Naturally, they are coming to me, asking, should I sign a lease, should I do this, should I do that? They are worried about their jobs. And they'll worry even more when they see what Snyder has done in Washington. I hope there is no way that will happen here. But you never know. The people here know that every single one of them might be affected, and that concern won't change until the next guy is in place and we all see what he wants to do here.

The organization is not in the best of situations. We don't own our stadium and we don't have the favorable lease with regards to money from luxury boxes and preferred seating that other franchises have. The important thing will be whether this owner wants to compete or not. I have some friends in the car racing business, and they tell me that some teams really want to compete, the others just want to drive around the track.

There are a lot of teams in this league that have been just driving around the track for twenty or thirty years, it is just not a case of bad luck here or there. You've earned it when you've been a loser that long.

There's no one way to do it at the ownership level. Green Bay has been perhaps the most successful franchise in the history of the NFL and they're run by a board of directors. In the end, motivation to win is what counts.

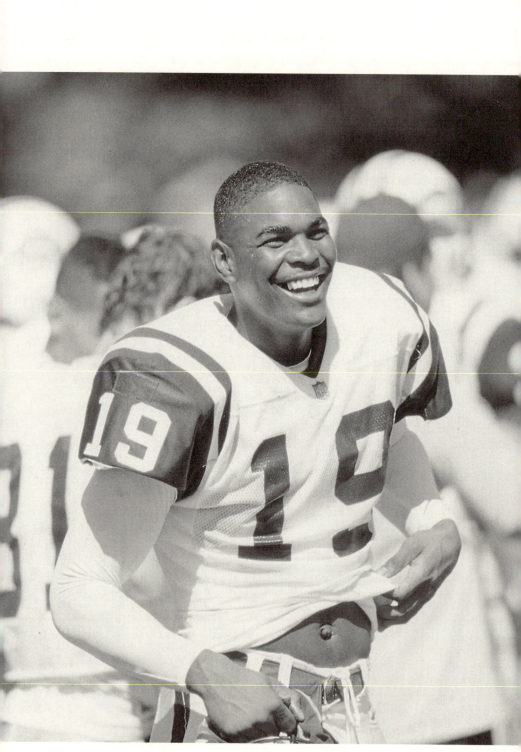

Keyshawn Johnson

LATE JULY 1999

Training camp hasn't even opened yet, but the season has started. Two of my players, Jumbo Elliott and Jason Fabini, our starting offensive tackles and very important guys on our team, have been arrested. The press is all over it, and I don't blame them. These were just a couple of guys being stupid. Going someplace they shouldn't have gone, and ending up in a brawl. I've talked to both of the players. They claim they are innocent. Do I believe their story 100 percent? Of course not. But do I believe what I'm reading in the papers about it? Of course not. Somewhere in the middle will be the truth.

For years, every time I have seen something in the paper, or on the Internet, about NFL players getting in trouble, I take it and read it to my team the very next day. I tell them, "Here is what is happening out there, fellas. It can happen to you. Do not go anywhere you are not known or not welcome." I emphasize it constantly. Ninety percent of this stuff happens in nightclubs, just like this one did.

Now the story these two guys give me is that they were out in a local nightclub celebrating with one of our former players, Matt O'Dwyer, who was a starting guard with us last year. In the middle of last season we offered O'Dwyer an $8 million contract over four years. He and his agent said it wasn't enough. That he's a $3.5 million-a-year ballplayer. We didn't think so. No one else did either. He signed in Cincinnati as a free agent for $3.5

million over two years. That averages out to $1.75 million a year for two years, less than what we offered him. The irony is that the three of them went out to celebrate O'Dwyer's new contract in Cincinnati.

My two players tell me they were some distance from O'Dwyer in the nightclub when the ruckus started. They said they went over to where he was to break up the fight, and the thing erupted into a melee. My players say they were not fighting. I think Fabini, from the looks of things right now, was just a bystander. There were no alcohol charges brought against them, so I have to assume they were not drunk. But since they're not average guys, in these situations they become targets of lawsuits. I told them how disappointed I was in both of them. Their conduct in this is embarrassing to the New York Jets as an organization and to me personally as the head coach. These players know better than that, and if they are found guilty, I will fine them, maybe some game checks, which will amount to a lot of money. I'm sure if they are found guilty in court, the league will fine them as well. If they are acquitted I don't think there will be any fines from either the team or the league.

I've been lucky that I haven't had a lot of this kind of thing during my coaching career. When I was in New England our best running back my first year there, Leonard Russell, got stabbed outside a nightclub and was damn near killed. With the Giants I had some guys picked up for driving under the influence, or other traffic violations, but I haven't had too many assaults and things of that nature.

This kind of stuff seems to happen around the league at this time of year, the six- or seven-week break from the end of minicamp to the start of training camp. This is when the players are out of your sight for a long period of time, and this is bad news for some of these guys. As a coach you worry about drugs and the league testing at the opening of camp.

Ten, fifteen years ago, there were some teams in the league destroyed by drugs. It's pretty well documented that drugs ruined some Charger teams, and years after the fact, Tampa Bay said some of their early teams were ruined by them as well. In my eight years with the Giants we had thirty-four players treated. Most of it was at the start of my coaching there, until I got a handle on it. I think it was my second year as head coach with the Giants I put myself in a place called Fair Oaks in Summit, New Jersey, as an outpatient. I wanted to find out exactly what the problems were and how they were going to be treated. I felt that if I wanted to know as much as I could about drugs, and how to help my players, then I better learn everything about it. At Fair Oaks I worked with a terrific woman named Jane Jones. She dealt with a lot of our players. She was a tremendous resource for me in telling me how to deal with these players. I didn't do all I could. I wish I could have done more, but I did try to educate myself about drugs as best I could because I knew if I didn't, it was going to cost me and my coaches our careers.

In my opinion the drug problems in the league today are not as big as those days. Now I'm not so naive as to think that there still aren't some drugs around. I just think the league is a lot tougher and more thorough. And the Players Association seems to realize that a player's life is more important than trying to protect his job. I've seen a tremendous downswing in the use of recreational drugs like cocaine and marijuana in the last ten years. The league has been good about informing the players about its drug policy and disciplinary measures. It's not an easy thing to control. New drugs are coming on the market all the time, and there are different and more sophisticated ways to mask the drugs. I had a few problem players in New England, and a couple here with the Jets. Drugs have power. They are addictive, seductive, and they can take down the strongest people. I've seen it happen.

When I was with the Giants I had this kid who had everything going for him. Smart. Handsome. He had talent. I thought he could be something special, but he had this problem with cocaine. I had him sent to two rehabs. I took him to one of them personally and spent some time with him there. I always believed that if a player had a drug problem that I'd do every-thing in my power to help him get clean, and if he didn't want to go along, I was going to get rid of him. I did it myself. I didn't leave it up to the front office, or my assistant coaches. I'm a very hands-on coach in all areas, especially if there is a problem with a player.

Anyway, this guy played pretty well his first year for us and I had high hopes for him, but then he slipped up again. He just couldn't help himself. This stuff had control of him. I had to let him go. The day I had to tell him, we were both crying like babies in my office. It was a sad day. He was in way over his head. I thought that day I would never see this kid alive again, that someday I'd read in the newspaper that he was dead. When he was walking out the door he turned and said to me: "Coach, you did all you could do. Right now, this just has me." I never heard anything about him for years. He could have been dead for all I knew. But about two years ago I found out what hap-pened. He was into drugs for a long time after and tried but failed to make another team. Eventually he somehow turned his life around. He's a minister in the Atlanta area. He has his own church and is drug free.

The start of every training camp is different. You think you know what you have at the end of the spring minicamp, both individually and as a team. There is only one guy I was upset at when minicamp was over. Keyshawn Johnson. We had fifty-nine veteran players in our off-season program, and he was the only one who failed to finish. Fifty-eight guys did forty work-outs, except one. Keyshawn Johnson. He did thirty-two. I like this kid as a player. I didn't know what to expect from him when I first got here. He was the first player taken in the entire draft the year before, and he had a disappointing season. A lot of peo-ple thought he was a bust. We determined he was way over-weight at that time. He played at 220-something pounds, but when he was at USC he weighed 208. So I talked to him. "Look, this is working against you. You need to get your weight down."

The first year he was fighting it. I gave him a target weight of 210. It was hard for him, but he did it and had a good season. Last year, he had no problem with it and had a great season.

I have to listen to agents every year about what is important for their player. Keyshawn's agent, Jerome Stanley, is no exception. I tell him, "If you want me to listen to what is important to you and to Keyshawn, you have to listen to what is important to me." There's a kind of trade-off. I do the same thing with my team as a whole. Keyshawn was looking for a new big deal. He wanted to restructure the old one and get a lot more money. We were going to do it for him. Then he missed the eight workouts. That has changed things. He's not going to get the deal he thought he was going to get, and any deal we give him in the future will include mandatory workouts. They will be in the contract. I believe that these off-season workouts mean as much to team unity as just about anything else we do. It forces these players to interact with one another. You acquire respect for your teammate by watching him work.

Let me give a couple of examples of what happened this off-season. Vinny Testaverde had a big year for us last season. Played great, went to the Pro Bowl, and deserved it. Vinny lives in Florida and has a gym in his house. The guy is a well-conditioned athlete. I have no reservations about him getting in shape on his own. He's done it for years. When we started to talk about a new contract with him after the season, I told him, "If you don't come to our off-season program here, I don't want you to sign this contract. Don't sign it. That's how important it is to me." Vinny understood. He said, "Okay, I'll work it out." So he went out and chartered an airplane. Each week for ten weeks he flew up here, worked out for four days, and then flew back to Florida. He knew how important that was to me.

Let's take Bryan Cox. Bryan was a controversial player in Miami and Chicago. And we were questioned when we picked him up during training camp a year ago. But he's been a real professional ever since. In the middle of our off-season program—he had two weeks to finish—his wife became sick, and he had to return home. By the time she was okay again, our camp was over. But this guy still came back and finished the two weeks on his own, after everyone else was done.

I haven't seen Keyshawn since the end of minicamp. When he gets here, I'm going to talk to him and tell him how disappointed I am with what he did.

Other than that, I think this might be the best-conditioned team I have ever had coming into any training camp. Not one of our rookies failed any of our conditioning tests. I hope the same thing happens when they come back. If they don't pass, I'll deal with it. My first year in New England I had a guard named Reggie Redding. He had started the year before. He came into camp twenty-two pounds overweight. I just cut him right on the spot. When they're that far out of shape, why even bother. By showing up like that, they're telling you that they don't care enough.

Last year I had two guys miss our conditioning run by just a couple of seconds. So when the morning practice was over, I took them aside and gave them some "gassers" or a few "up and downs." The guys that have the toughest time with this are the big guys, the three-hundred-pound linemen. Being big myself I know how difficult some of these tests can be, but to me they are important. Since they have just finished a full morning practice, you have to be careful with these big guys when you condition them so they can pass the test. You don't want to kill them. They'll have to practice again in the afternoon.

I condition them myself. I don't leave it to the trainers or assistant coaches. A single "gasser" (some might call them wind sprints) is four times across the field, over and back. I want them to do it in thirty-seven or thirty-eight seconds. For a skill, or smaller player, I'll bring it down to thirty-six or thirty-five seconds. Then I'll throw in a few "up and downs," which is what Vince Lombardi was famous for. (My father knew Vince Lombardi, another Jersey guy. The Lombardi family lived in our neighborhood, and I played in the streets with Vince Jr. when we were kids. When I first became head coach of the Giants,

Vince Jr.'s kids were ball boys for me.) The player stands in place, running as fast as he can, lifting his knees as high as he can, then when I blow the whistle, he hits the ground as fast as he can. Sort of like a belly flop. He has to put his hands out to break the fall. I think there was a method to Vince's madness. In those days they didn't lift a lot of weights like we do now. This drill makes you develop your forearm and chest muscles.

I keep a close eye on these guys when I am working them out like that. I don't want them to collapse. I let them go back in, and I point them toward the cold pool, a big tub filled with cold water (about forty-four degrees). These pools are great for restoring muscles after practice. They cool the muscles right down. A lot of players go in and take a full dip. Others just stand up in them. We can put fifteen to twenty guys in there at one time. Sometimes I go in there myself.

Overall I feel pretty good waiting for them to come in. I think we've improved our defense by picking up Steve Atwater to play safety for us and Roman Phifer to help as a linebacker. If we stay healthy we should be better. I'm worried about our defensive line in terms of depth and quality. I want to work in some of our young people there. I've got two or three second-year guys that need to play well to give us depth.

Offensively, I think we are very good at center and at tackle, and with Eric Green coming in, we have upgraded at tight end. My biggest concern is at guard, where we have two openings. O'Dwyer is gone and so is Todd Burger, who had some problems I didn't want to deal with and a performance level that wasn't good enough. I need to find a couple of guys that will step up.

Our wide receivers are pretty good. I expect Dedric Ward to have a big season. He's been getting better each year. He made some big plays coming down the stretch for us last year. He put the game away for us with a long touchdown catch in an important win against New England, and then had another long catch for the winning score in Buffalo late in the season. We have three—Keyshawn, Dedric, and Wayne Chrebet—who are very good. I'd like to pick up a fourth guy I can count on. We thought about grabbing Quinn Early, who played in Buffalo and has been a reliable veteran.

Our punting should be better with Tom Tupa. He can play quarterback as well, and that will set up some good competition with Scott Zolak and Ray Lucas. We've got a place kicker, John Hall, who has about the strongest leg in the league. On kickoffs, the guy is a weapon. On field goals, you are never sure where the ball is going to go when it leaves his foot. He made a lot of improvement from his first to second year, and if he continues to improve this year, he should be fine.

I'm a superstitious guy though. When this fight happened with Fabini and Elliott, I wondered if it was a bad omen. A sign of things to come. I remember a night or two before my third training camp in New England. We had a surprising finish the year before to make the playoffs, and I felt very good about our chances for the upcoming season. Then my phone rang at home, and my security guy up in New England starts telling me I got a problem. The night before, one of our guys was picked up jogging along Route 1, not too far from our stadium in Foxborough. Around midnight, the police stopped him because they didn't think he was dressed appropriately. As a matter of fact, he wasn't dressed at all. The only thing he wore were his sneakers. Not a stitch of clothing. Not even socks. This kid was a rookie free agent. We hadn't researched him that well. If he was one of our draft choices, there's a good chance we would have found out that he had some severe mental problems. That day he was gone. It didn't take long. He didn't have a lot to pack.

We ended up having a disappointing season that year in New England, with a 6–10 record.

AUGUST 1, 1999

The greatest player I ever coached went into the Hall of Fame on July 31, 1999. Unfortunately, the media around here is trying to make me part of the story. "Aren't you offended that Lawrence didn't ask you to present him?" I told them no, but some of them didn't want to listen to that. They had to put their own spin on it. "Shouldn't you have really been in Canton, Ohio, for the ceremony rather than coaching your team here?" The answer to that one is no as well.

Lawrence and I talked about this sometime back, before he was even elected to the Hall. At the time he was acting like there was no question he would be voted in, and if he wasn't, it wouldn't be any big deal. But there was a question about him getting in due to his drug problems of the past, and he was worried about that publicity hurting his chances. At one point he even asked me straight out, "Do you think I'm going to get in?" I assured him that he would because he deserved it. He always told me that if he ever did become a Hall of Famer, he wanted me to present him. Later though he told me, "I'm going to let my son do it." I told him that was a great idea. It didn't bother me at all, and still doesn't.

Lawrence visited our camp six or seven days before he went to Canton for the induction. We spent the morning together, talking about a lot of things. He told me that I would be in his

Lawrence Taylor. The greatest.

heart, and that I would be there with him in spirit. He said he was grateful for what I had done for him.

Well, let me tell you what Lawrence Taylor did for me. I wouldn't be sitting where I am today without him. He was the major reason for our winning with the New York Giants. This guy is a very special player, and I never had another one like him. Without question he is the best player I ever had the good fortune to coach. He was totally unselfish, and I never saw him do a malicious thing on the football field. He played as hard as he possibly could, but he never took a cheap shot at anyone, even though I saw a lot taken at him. When something happened he handled it well. He would respond verbally, but he never overreacted.

Above all, Lawrence changed the way the game is played, and when a player has the ability to do that, and does it, then he certainly is a Hall of Fame player. He was dominant, relentless. If you were the team playing against him, you just couldn't leave him alone in space. You had to account for him with one, two, and sometimes three guys. And when you did that, then he changed the way the team would normally play the game. Lawrence raised havoc with the other teams' offenses. His speed and power were just too much for any one person in the league to try to block. I saw him totally disrupt what some teams wanted to do. He made some of the most amazing plays in the history of the NFL, right up to the end of his career.

And not only was he very durable, but he would also play in pain. He suited up for a game in Denver with a broken ankle. He gave it three plays but couldn't go on. Another night in New Orleans, in a very important game, he played with a separated shoulder that kept popping in and out, but he refused to come out of the game. It was the most courageous thing I have ever seen on a football field.

I have two great stories about Lawrence that I love to tell people. The first was during a game against the St. Louis Cardinals when he was a rookie. We had a defensive formation where Lawrence was supposed to drop back into pass coverage. During the play, instead of dropping into coverage, he attacked the quarterback and sacked him. When he came to the sideline I told him, "Look, we went over this in practice. You know what they are going to do on third down and you are supposed to be covering the receiver on the out pattern."

"Oh, I got it. I got it," he said, nodding his head.

"This is going to come up again, so pay attention," I said. "I'm going to call the same defensive play. Execute it."

Sure enough, about ten minutes later, the same situation comes up: third down, seven or eight yards to go, and I call the defense. They run the same play. He rushes again, hits the quarterback, the ball is fumbled, and George Martin picks it up and runs for a touchdown. So Lawrence now has two plays where he does the wrong thing and sacks the quarterback both times, one for a touchdown. After the play, all of his teammates are pounding him on the back and congratulating him, but when he comes to the bench and sees me, he says, "I did it again, didn't I?"

I told him it was a dumb play, and we don't even have a play where he was supposed to do what he did. When I told him that, he looked at me and smiled, saying, "We'd better put it in Monday, Bill, because it's a dandy." True story.

The other story starts with Joe Gibbs and the Redskins. Gibbs decided his problem with trying to beat us was Lawrence, so if he could find a way to neutralize Lawrence, then he could win. In this one game, Gibbs gave some help to Joe Jacoby, who was a hell of an offensive tackle and a Pro Bowl player—but he couldn't handle Lawrence one-on-one. Gibbs put not only the tight end over on Jacoby's side, but also his wingback for most of the game. Three players to handle Lawrence. Believe it or not, they were successful. Lawrence didn't make a single tackle. The problem for them was we won the game, 21–10.

After the game, the press kept asking, "What's wrong with Taylor?" I tried to explain that the Redskins were double- and triple-teaming him. The next week we played San Diego, and Dan Henning, who is now the quarterback coach here on my staff, was the head coach of the Chargers. Dan, who had coached in

Washington under Gibbs before taking the San Diego job, looked at what Gibbs had done and decided he wasn't going to let Lawrence make any plays either. So he double- and triple-teamed him, too. Lawrence made only one tackle. But again we won the game. The press started again. "What's wrong with Taylor?"

We played Minnesota next. The week leading up to the game, I would get on Lawrence a little bit during practice.

"You know, Taylor," I said. "I'm going to change your name to What's the Matter." So all week long I called him What's the Matter. It was funny for about a day. Then the other players picked up on it. I knew Lawrence was starting to get mad, but I kept it up anyway.

We played the Vikings on Monday Night Football. They had Tommy Kramer at quarterback and they were playing well. Phil Simms got hurt on the first play of the game, but still we ended up winning, 24–10, thanks to Lawrence. He was a one-man show. The Vikings decided to leave him in space, try to block him with just one guy. At the end of the game, he had nine tackles, two and a half sacks, and he caused two fumbles.

It was a big win for us because I think both teams were about 8–1 at the time. About an hour after the game I was talking with the Vikings coach Jerry Burns outside of the locker room. All of a sudden something jumped on my back from behind. It was Taylor, still in uniform. As he was riding me piggyback he leaned over and looked in my face and said, "They're not asking you what's the matter with Taylor tonight, are they?"

Now that was a case where I used the media to help me. Most of the time, I try to help them, though it isn't always easy. In fact, I meet with reporters more than I have to. I give them one extra day each week, and many times during my career I went out of my way to help some of them out when I didn't have to. I also believe that you can't have fifteen different guys in your organization talking about what is going on, which is why I subscribe to One Voice, my own personal philosophy.

I've seen other organizations allow their assistant coaches to talk to the media, and it ends up being divisive to the whole organization. Anyone can say the wrong thing, and if an assistant coach, who doesn't know what is going on inside the organization, makes a comment that is incorrect, we have a problem. I don't want any problems that I can avoid, so I tell my assistants not to talk. I talk. Then if there's a problem, it's one I created for myself.

I started to think this way when I was with the Giants. The owners were tight-lipped. George Young, the general manager, didn't talk too much about the football program. He talked about his own domain and stayed away from coaching. I liked the way that worked. Then I went to New England and found the opposite. They had too many guys talking before I got there, all telling different stories. All of them had cultivated friends in the media and were using them to get the word out to cover their own backsides. It was like an infestation. They were behaving like novices, and it destroyed the organization. When I took over New England I made sure that wasn't going to happen again. I spoke both as a coach and a general manager with control over the personnel department.

I've taken the same approach here with the Jets. One voice. I do all of the talking. And one of the first things I try to do is figure out where all of the guys I am dealing with in the media on a daily basis are coming from, what they are trying to accomplish. I can usually figure out their agenda by the questions they ask me. My answers are then based on what my experience is with the reporter and what I think he or she is after. I appreciate those that work hard, do their homework, and come prepared. People who are organized and efficient. They have my respect. If a guy is trying to do a good job and report things in a credible and objective way, I'll go out of my way to help him out. Then there are other reporters who come in here, particularly in the electronic media, that try to antagonize you, looking for a sound bite. They want a reaction that will give them some good tape. You can sense it by the question. Some days I give them what they want, others I don't. It all depends on my mood. One of the hard things from my side is figuring out whether the editors are juicing these people they send out to cover the team in a certain way, or if it's the reporters' own way of doing business.

I don't know what is happening inside a newspaper or a television station or a radio station. Some of the stuff you hear on the radio shows nowadays is so far-out, so distorted and removed from the truth, it makes you wonder how it started in the first place. Then these people bring it into a press conference and start asking questions and preface it with something like: "People are saying. . . ." What people? Talk show people. Like I'm supposed to answer to some ridiculous story or rumor that started with some guy calling in on a talk show.

Honestly, there are times I use the media. I don't say I would contrive a whole scenario, but I have enough experience to know that if I make a certain comment, how the press will react to it, and what will happen as a result. Sometimes I use them to send a message to my team. Rather than bending the players' ears all the time, man-to-man, I might say something to the media early in the week like, "If we don't throw the ball better this week, we're not going to win." The quarterback reads that and you can see in his eyes the rest of the week he is pissed and wants to prove something.

One time with the Giants, I planted a message by saying, "If we don't stop John Riggins running inside this week, we don't have a chance." Riggins was having a big year running the ball for Washington. We had a tackle named Jim Burt, and the comment was meant for him. He stuffed Riggins, and we won something like 37–13. He hasn't let me forget it since. To this day, when I see him, he still brings it up.

I never use the media if I've got a problem with a player. When that happens, I bring him into my office and we talk about it directly. That's how Lawrence and I dealt with this whole Hall of Fame thing. Directly. That's the way it has always been with us. He knows that through all the problems he has had, and during everything we've been through, I have tried to do the right thing for him. We have always stayed close, and always will, because he knows that even when I got on his ass pretty good about things, I was on his side. I love the guy like he was one of my own kids. Now, sometimes, that has been tough love. Two or three times over the years we came close to blows.

Taylor knew how good he was, and he liked to talk a lot. Sometimes we'd go at it verbally on the practice field, and sometimes it got hot. I'd be yelling. He'd be yelling. We'd get in each other's face. Sometimes I belted him on the shoulder pads. A couple of times I told him, "If you just shut up and do what you're told, we'd be a lot better off." You got the best out of Taylor when you challenged him.

One time we went into Washington for a big game, and I could see he was more nervous than usual. Not nervous afraid. Nervous waiting for the game to happen. He loved big games. He always seemed to play great in Washington. Joe Gibbs said I always made something up about the Redskins before the game—like they thought Taylor was horseshit, or didn't respect him, or thought he was overrated—because Taylor killed them.

On this particular day, I walked over to him just before the game and said, "Am I gonna have to worry about you today, too?" He got pissed. "Don't worry about me. Worry about those other sons of bitches you got on this team because I know what I'm going to do." His eyes could have burned a hole in me. They were jumping out of his head.

As a player, Lawrence never let me down. He was always there for me. And I'll always be there for him. No matter how big his problems are I will never count him out. He told me when we talked last week, "Bill, I'm putting my life back together, piece by piece. But right now, I've only got the job about half done." He knows he's got more work to do, and if he needs me, I'll be right there with him.

AUGUST 25, 1999

We're halfway through preseason and I'm not a happy camper. I'm very concerned about this team and I've told them that. Right now we seem to have an overinflated opinion of ourselves, and that can be a team killer.

We lost to Green Bay in the preseason opener, but I wasn't bothered by that. When both first teams played against each other, we had the better of it, which is not easy to do in Green Bay. Lambeau Field is the best place to take a team in the preseason. It's almost always sold out. The fans are enthusiastic, and the atmosphere is just like a regular season game. No matter what, the fans stay to the end. In the second half we gave them something to stick around for. We were awful. We couldn't do a thing on offense, and I was very disappointed in the play of Ray Lucas. I really like this kid. He's a good athlete, and a good competitor. I was hoping he would show me something where he could be the backup behind Vinny Testaverde. But he had a bad night, and his execution wasn't great. In fairness to him, he had a bunch of guys around him who were inexperienced. As a result we dropped eight passes, had four sacks against us, and we got flagged for eight offensive penalties.

Green Bay had the better backups playing, and in the second half they handled us easily to get the win. Matt Hasselbeck, who used to be a ball boy for us when his dad, Don, played tight end for me with the Giants, played quarterback for them and had a

An old friend Ron Wolf, general manager for the Packers, visiting me during camp. I traded for Rick Mirer with him.

great second half. He threw a couple of touchdown passes, and they scored twenty unanswered points.

Our second preseason game was last week at home against Philadelphia. We won, but we played worse than we did in Green Bay. It was a miserable night, with rain and half the seats empty. We won, 10–9, and that's the best thing I can say about it. Vinny had a decent game, passing 11 for 14. Our defense was okay, but our special teams stunk. Just awful. They couldn't do anything right.

So I told the team when we got together for practice this week, that if we keep on going the way we are going, we're not going to win anything this year. I don't like our attitude.

From the players' body language and the way they were acting I knew before the game in Philly that we weren't prepared to play. They thought there was no way they could lose to Philly. They acted cool, like they could give a shit. They were lethargic, moving in slow motion. When a team has respect for another team, you can feel it in the fear factor. You can sense it on the field before the game. We didn't have any respect for the Eagles. Our guys didn't think they had much of a club. And as a result, we played like dogs. This was leftover from the year before. We were the big guys that almost went to the Super Bowl. They were a bad team in a bad division.

There isn't a team in this league that you can play against and feel that way. That only leads to trouble. These guys seem to think this team can turn it on and off anytime it feels like it. That's not even close to being correct.

When I coached the Giants, I had a couple of teams that thought they were great when they weren't. We paid the price in the end. In 1989, it caused our Giants to lose games we shouldn't have lost. Then we came down to the final game of the season, against the Jets. If we won, we had the division and a spot in the playoffs, so there was a lot on the line. We went into the fourth quarter of the game and blew it. We lost the game and the division, and we didn't get to the playoffs. Right then and there I knew there were some veterans on the team who had to go. I singled out the veterans because rookies rarely have bad attitudes. They just want a job in the league to make some money. Veterans, though, especially the backups, can be a different story. They know after being around a few years they're not good enough, but they don't want to accept that. They bitch and moan and make excuses. Sometimes they get bad attitudes because of their contracts. Money is a big thing now. It's a topic of conversation in the locker room. If some of these players see another guy is sensitive about being a backup, or not getting enough playing time, or his contract, then they start to stick the needles in pretty good. Once I feel a player has a bad attitude, for whatever reason, I look to get rid of him the first chance I get. I won't do it to hurt the ball club. If the guy can contribute, or is the best we can get at that time, I keep him around, but I'll be looking for someone better. The wrong attitude cost us the whole season in '89, and I sense this thing happening here now, and I'm trying to put a stop to it.

Of course, you've got to have a standard to compare all of this to. For me, it was the 1990 Giants, a team that was the best I ever had in terms of knowing what it had to do to win. They realized early on that we had a good defensive team, but we weren't going to score a lot of points on offense. They played that way all year. We were great at winning the close ball games. Three points, six points, we won them. If we had a lead going into the fourth period, we held it. If we needed a score in the fourth period, we got it. This approach helped us go all the way that year.

Against the 49ers in San Francisco in the Conference Championship game, we looked like we were dead. San Francisco had the lead and the ball, running out the clock. Then our defense turned it over and we got the ball back, and moved it up the field for Matt Bahr to kick the winning field goal with time running out. (Matt has the courage of a lion. I'd rather have him try to kick the winning field goal for me with the game on the line than any other kicker I have ever seen.) In the Super

Bowl, against a good Buffalo team, we were underdogs. But we did what we had to do. We knew we had to control the ball on offense, which we did, and not let them make a big play on offense. Then Scott Norwood missed the field goal for the Bills, and we won. Every one of those Giants players knew what it took to win.

Now I'm at the point where there isn't much I can do except grind them. Sunday we had a hard practice. Then Monday, we had the two toughest practices of the year. We had contact. We got some guys nicked up, but I didn't care. I'm trying to wake them up. They've got to get back on track or we won't go anywhere. We've got to reestablish our edge here.

When I want to get a team's attention, we scrimmage. At any level of football, if you want to bust players' humps, you scrimmage. You make them hit. Players hate it, but they understand it if they have a brain in their head. Their fear is injury. Mine is, too. But this is still a physical game, and if they don't get the job done during a game, you make sure they get their share of hitting in during the week. If the team is on a roll and winning, you back off. You cut them some slack. You take the pads off in practice. You cut down the contact. A team can be mentally fatigued as well. I guard against it all the time. If I'm tired, then I start to look closer at them, and most of the time, they're tired as well. So I give them some time off. In football you'd rather err on the side of less, rather than more. You don't want to go into a game with a tired team.

I don't want to push them too far, so I have my own little formula for figuring out how much is enough. I know who the best one or two conditioned athletes on my team are, and I gauge them. In New England I had a wide receiver named Shawn Jefferson who could run all day. You couldn't get him tired. He was unreal. If I saw him dragging a bit, then I knew it was time to back off with the rest of the team. If he was dragging, the rest of them had to be a lot worse.

•   •   •

I traded for Rick Mirer from Green Bay. Backup quarterback Scott Zolak didn't turn out the way I had hoped, so I let him go. It wasn't the best timing for the team. I could have used him to fill in the rest of the preseason in case someone gets hurt, but I like him so much personally, and letting him go now gives him a better chance to hook on with someone else. Scott just couldn't do it. I watched him through all of our practices, and he didn't throw with the accuracy I had hoped for, and he lacked mobility. Between the way Scott was practicing and the way Ray Lucas played in Green Bay, I felt I had to get a seasoned guy with playing experience who could step up in case something happens to Vinny.

Green Bay had four quarterbacks and I knew they wouldn't keep all four, and they weren't going to get rid of Brett Favre. Besides Mirer and Hasselbeck, they also have Aaron Brooks, a young quarterback that my friend Ron Wolf, the Packers general manager, is very high on.

When we got back from Green Bay I called Ron and asked him about Mirer. I thought he might be expendable because he is older and carries a much bigger salary than the other two kids. Ron wanted to wait another week and see how they did in practice. When it was over he called me and we made the deal. It wasn't in Green Bay's best interest to do it at this time either, should someone get hurt, but I asked him to do it now so we could get Mirer started in learning our system. So far, in just a couple of days of practice, I like what I see. He's throwing the ball well, and he has mobility.

We thought about drafting Rick out of Notre Dame when I was in my first year coaching New England. We had the first pick in the draft, and we needed a quarterback. Besides Rick, Drew Bledsoe was coming out of Washington State. We studied both of them intensely. In the end we decided to take Drew because he could make all of the throws, and we didn't think Rick could. Drew had the bigger arm that could get the ball anywhere on the field. Rick was more of a play-action guy. He had better mobility and, at the time, more poise because he had played in more pressure-packed games than Drew. Age was also a factor: Drew was only twenty. Rick was twenty-three. Seattle took Rick as the second pick in the draft.

San Francisco had been very interested in making a trade for the first pick. They told me they wanted Mirer. Bill Walsh had finished up with San Francisco and was calling Notre Dame games on television for NBC, and he fell in love with Rick. He thought he would make a great pro and compared him favorably to another Notre Dame quarterback, Joe Montana. Walsh had the 49ers convinced this was the way to go. They offered me their entire draft that year, seven picks, but I didn't do it. If I did, we wouldn't have had a quarterback, and I was hoping Drew could be a big-time player in the future. It turned out that way.

Rick was the rookie of the year in the AFC that first season. He started in Seattle for three years, but his team never got any better. He didn't either. Drew started to get a better team around him, and he continued to improve his game. Rick was traded to Chicago, which was closer to his home. This is just about the worst thing that could have happened to him. Players generally feel an added sense of pressure playing for their home team. And the coach, Dave Wannstadt, was fighting to keep his job. This deal didn't turn out well for Rick. It would have been tough for anyone to be successful under those circumstances. He then went to Green Bay and was behind Favre. Brett doesn't get hurt. He's been the iron man quarterback in the league the last three years.

Injuries are starting to bother our team. We haven't lost anyone for the season, but we've got a bunch of guys who are out for two and three weeks. For some guys, it might be just too bad. Ernie Logan, a veteran defensive lineman, got hurt in the Philadelphia game and will be out for a couple of weeks. That might be it for him. I didn't like the way he was playing before he got hurt, and when we get down to making the final cuts, he could be on the list.

We have eighty guys with us, but in my mind I have the squad cut to about fifty-eight. I know forty-three guys who are going to be with us for sure, unless they get hurt. We can keep fifty-three. That means fifteen guys are going to be fighting for ten spots over the final two preseason games.

It's an ongoing evaluation. When I look at a player for talent, I try to see him playing his position, and I ask myself, "Who does he remind me of?" I say this guy looks like so and so, and plays like so and so. I try to visualize the player. In golf they tell you to visualize your shot before you strike the ball. As a coach, I see a player and I try to see him making the plays at his position. And if the guy doesn't look like anyone I've had in my coaching career, then in my opinion that guy isn't any good. I get a kick when people say about some kid, "He's the next Lawrence Taylor." Well, I haven't ever seen anyone and said that. There are a lot of guys who were supposed to be Lawrence Taylors in bus stations all over the country.

I'm not happy with Leon Johnson. He's a talented back who had a very good rookie year for us, then got injured last year. I think he's on cruise control. Some guys look like world-beaters until they make the team and get some security. Then they don't play with quite the same intensity. Johnson can still do it when he has the ball under his arm, but when he doesn't have the ball, whether it's blocking or on special teams, he's a disappointment. He hasn't been doing a good job on special teams, and if he continues to go bad on us, it will hurt the team. We count on him being on the field thirty-five or forty plays a game.

Developing depth has become a problem. In the off-season tight end Johnny Mitchell came to me and told me he just wanted a chance to play again.

The guy turned out to be a phony. That's been his problem. He left Nebraska when he was just twenty years old, and the Jets made him a first-round pick in 1992. From what I've heard from the people who were here at the time and are still around now, he was very immature when it came to football. He had the talent, but he didn't know how to get the most out of it. He played three or four years here and they let him go. Dallas picked him up and he played just a handful of games. He dropped out of football for a couple of years and tried catching on with the Dolphins, but they didn't bring him back. Then he came to us looking for another chance. The guy is talented and we needed some help at tight end, so when he called me, I gave him a shot. We also gave him some money. He came here and worked out the forty days and did everything we asked him to do. Then after the very first day of training camp, he quit. One day. He left without seeing me. He just took off. We gave him a workout bonus, so I'm going to try to get that back. His agent said he would help us get that done. In my opinion, the guy didn't have the heart for football or to do what it takes to be a great player. I'm sorry I ever gave him the shot.

Ten-year veteran Erik Norgard quit the same day, but his was a different story. He was a veteran offensive lineman with Tennessee who we thought could help us. We signed him as a free agent with a $300,000 contract. He practiced three times and decided it was time to retire. He came to me and said he was going to retire because he just didn't want to play anymore. He gave us our bonus back. Players sometimes get to a point where they are facing two practices a day in training camp and they simply don't want to go through it anymore. I respect Norgard for the way he handled the situation. He was a gentleman about it, very respectful and very cooperative.

When Mitchell left we needed another tight end H-back type player, so we brought Keith Byars back to the team. I told him in the spring to stay prepared in case anything happened, because he'd be the first guy I called. Keith is comfortable with me and our system. This guy is one of the truly great unsung players of all time. He's a total professional. I gained great respect for him when I was coaching the Giants and he was playing for some very good Philadelphia teams. The guy didn't make mistakes. He was hard-nosed. He ran, he blocked, he caught the ball. He played several positions. His number one priority was winning, not stats. I picked him up in New England when he was cut by Miami for salary cap reasons. He came in on a Wednesday and helped us win a game in Indianapolis the next Sunday. He played three different positions: running back, wingback, and tight end. He played over twenty plays and didn't make a single mental error. He is a student of the game.

When Norgard left, we brought in Ian Beckles, who had played in Tampa Bay. This is the kind of situation you have to be prepared for in the off-season. We compile a big list for every position. We call the top guys who are still available and tell them they'll get the first call if a position opens up. I also traded with the San Diego Chargers for John Burke, a tight end I had when I was in New England. He gives me more insurance and is a good special teams player. I also brought in two veteran wide receivers, Quinn Early and Dwight Stone. I'm very happy with Keyshawn Johnson, Wayne Chrebet, and Dedric Ward, but I want someone to jump up and show he's a quality fourth guy.

I could also use another cornerback. Otis Smith, our starting right cornerback, broke his clavicle. During practice he was covering a deep pass and jumped for the ball. When he came down, he landed on his shoulder and it gave way. He won't be back until after the regular season starts. Blake Spence, a kid who I thought might make a big leap for us this year, has been hurt and out for a couple of weeks. Spence plays the F-back position, where he goes out for passes from the backfield and also provides lead blocking for the running back. Lawrence Hart, a tight end, got poked in the eye and is having vision problems.

It drives you crazy when you lose players, even when you know some of it has to happen. It's inevitable. But it bogs down the pace of your camp, and you can't progress the way you want to.

When Mitchell and Norgard packed up, I called the rest of the squad together and told them, "If any of you other guys want to quit, do it right now. I don't want you wasting my time or the other coaches' time. I'm too old to deal with this crap. Football isn't for everyone. It's not something shameful to say that you don't feel like playing anymore, so if you do, say it now."

No one moved.

We're playing the Giants this week, and they're pretty damn good. I've watched their film, and Kent Graham is really throwing the ball well. I think he's got that job won. This will be an important game for us. Either we'll keep on playing the way we have, or we'll start to come around and play the type of football this team is capable of playing.

*We lost Wayne Chrebet to a freak injury for the first few games,
which didn't help our offense.*

SEPTEMBER 7, 1999

It's 7:30 in the morning, the Tuesday before our regular season opening game at home this Sunday against New England. Personally, I'm a little tired. I'm falling back into that same old syndrome where I can't sleep. Last night I went to bed exhausted because I had a tough couple of days cutting some players I'm very fond of, and trying to make a deal to get another wide receiver.

Wayne Chrebet, one of our best offensive weapons, broke his foot in the last preseason game against Minnesota without getting hit. All he was doing was running out on a pass pattern, and the thing went on him. He'll be out for five or six weeks. Right now, opening the season, wide receiver is my biggest concern, which is why I am going to try to pick up someone from somewhere, anywhere, and get him in here before Sunday.

It's always on my mind. I fell asleep by 9:30. I woke up at 2:54. And I haven't slept since. I just lay there, thinking about the situation for hours until it got too boring. Then I came in here and got to work.

Yesterday was emotional because I had to release one of my favorite players, Corwin Brown, a backup safety. I love the guy. For six years, in New England and here with the Jets, he has given me everything he had. He's a tough kid and great on special teams. He's a foxhole guy, the kind you want to fight in the trenches with when you go to war. Corwin loves the game. I counted on him to play hard and play smart. It was very difficult to let Corwin go, but we signed Steve Atwater as a free agent and we have to get more out of the safety position than we did last year. Atwater is a Pro Bowl player. He's on the downside of his career, but I think he will improve the play at that position.

I told Corwin there's a time when you have to stop chasing the football and get on with the rest of your life. If another team doesn't take him, he's going to sit out the season, and then go into coaching. I told him there are a lot of people in his home state of Michigan and here who are ready to help him out. It isn't easy when I bring into my office someone who is like one of my children, sit him down, and give him the bad news. It gets a little teary at times. I'm cutting him loose from the family, and it gets to me.

I also had to release Keith Byars. In our final preseason game against Minnesota, he caught a touchdown pass and a two-point conversion. I wish I could keep him, but I can't. The Dolphins put Bernie Parmalee out on waivers, and I'm going to claim him later today. Bernie is young, makes less money, and is a great special teams player. This is a case where making too much money hurts a guy when you have to figure everything under the salary cap. If Keith made less money, he'd be here. I told him to stay in shape. If anything happens to any of our guys in the first couple of games, I'm going to bring him back.

People don't understand how close most of the teams in the NFL are. I wish the whole country could be inside our locker room. I'd love America to see how it can be. How we all interact with one another, regardless of what someone's color is, or what nationality they are. Black or white, it doesn't make a difference.

I'm not saying there still isn't some racism. There will be racism no matter where you go in society. But I think our locker room is pretty special. When you have a good team, the guys like one another, interact with one another as families, go to one another's houses for dinner, build strong friendships and wonderful bonds. When this happens, there are no secrets, no back-stabbing, everything is out in the open, and if there is a confrontation, it happens and then it is over.

This special bond happens because there is such a heavy physical price to pay in this game. Players need one another, and they know it. And they respect one another because of what they go through together doing this job. They also pull a lot of practical jokes—no one is safe from the locker room antics. It's this unusual closeness that makes it so hard for a guy like Corwin or Keith.

The game is such a big part of their lives. If they're not playing this season, after doing this for the last fifteen or twenty years, they are going to feel it.

We beat two good teams to wrap up the preseason, the Giants and Minnesota. I think the Giants might surprise some people. I think they have a chance to win their division. They are very good defensively, and they've got more weapons on offense than in the past.

We jumped on them at the start of the game, and it shouldn't have been close at the end, but it was. I liked this Giants game because it was like a regular season game, with about seventy thousand people in the stands. There's some feeling in New York because it's about bragging rights. And I wanted to show the Giants what kind of team we have, because we play them again during the regular season and we want them to know we can beat them.

Last year Baltimore came in here in the preseason and kicked our ass, 30–0. Not only was it embarrassing, but they also came back in and beat us a few weeks later during the regular season. I told our players that when you give a team the idea they can beat you the first time they play you in a season, chances are they'll do it again the second time.

I started Ray Lucas, which was a switch. My quarterbacks coach, Dan Henning, came up with the idea. Ray disappointed us when we played him in Green Bay, so Dan felt it was time to find out if he could do it under pressure. We didn't tell him he was going to start until we were in our hotel the night before the game. I wanted to do something to build his confidence a little bit, and he got us off with a great fourteen-play drive to score a touchdown. We didn't script the plays for him. We called them from the sidelines like we normally do, and he did a good job. He showed us he could respond to the pressure, then we got him out of there and went with our regular group.

Curtis Martin had a big game, running for over a hundred yards. Bryan Cox was great on defense, making eight tackles. We played a smart game. I think we had only six mental mistakes in the game. But we left eleven points on the field when Dedric Ward dropped a touchdown pass and our kicker missed an extra point and a field goal.

Then last week we played Minnesota in our last preseason game. This was one of the most dominant teams in the league last year. They lost only once in the regular season. They could go all the way this year, although their defense is not what I would call great. Offensively, now, they are exceptional. This is the biggest offensive team I have ever seen. Their offensive line is huge and good. Their tight end, Glover, is 6–6. Their three wide receivers—Moss, Carter, and Reed—are all 6–3 or better, and Randall Cunningham, their quarterback, is 6–4.

They are physically imposing and are a strong team, with good speed to the outside. Their defense plays a different style than most. We call it an undercover scheme. It is built around speed. They have smaller, quicker guys who can run to the ball. They put their defensive linemen in the gaps, rather than head-on, and want them to penetrate fast, to disrupt the blocking schemes. Then they have linebackers that can run, sort of slash their way to the ball.

They do not have good cornerbacks, though. And it is hard to play this kind of defense well without corners who can cover effectively. They had their way with us early in the game. They marched right down to score a touchdown the first time they touched the ball and went up, 7–0. The next time, they got a field goal and went up 10–3. Their defense was getting after Vinny and knocking him around. We weren't blocking them at all.

Fortunately for us, our defense held us in the game and gave us a chance to win, which we did, going away, 38–17. I was very happy about the game because Mirer completed his first five passes, with three of them for touchdowns. So I feel much better about my number two guy now than when I had Scott Zolak.

Vinny didn't have great stats in this game, but I told him later I thought he did a hell of a job. There were times he simply threw the ball away. There were other times when he took the hits to protect the ball. I told our whole team later that if we had made a critical mistake anywhere in that period of the game when they were ahead, 10–3, and we were struggling, then they would have beat us.

If you go behind 17–3 to an offensive powerhouse like that, chances aren't very good that you are coming back. But we didn't give up the big play, or the interception, or the fumble. We held on defense and started to chip away until we dominated the game in the second half.

This week The Crusade is coming to town, but it won't be like the last couple of years when we played New England. This is only a big game around Boston. Not in New York. And I think the Tuna Bowl stuff, or whatever they want to call this game, is starting to die out. I have no special feeling for this game, other than that I want to win it and get our season off to a good start.

Yes, the first two years after I left New England, I wanted to kick their butts. But after we beat them up there and down here last year, I don't think there is anything more to prove. They can beat us. We can beat them. And I don't dislike Pete Carroll. They're on his case up there this year, but I think he has done a good job, under difficult circumstances. In a way, I feel sorry for Pete. He is constantly being compared to what we did in New England. Deep down, he has to be tired of hearing my name. The couple of times I've talked to him since he took the job I told him that there wasn't anything personal with him as far as I was concerned. I had a little problem with Pete last year, but we got that straightened out.

He was quoted in a paper down here criticizing me, and he said later than it didn't come out the way he thought it would. I told him I'm a coach's guy, we should be loyal to one another as coaches, and none of us should be going around knocking one another.

We have to do something this week to take care of their wide receivers. They've got a bunch of good one: Terry Glenn, Shawn Jefferson, Troy Brown, Tony Simmons. Drew likes to look to Ben Coates first. Ben is his security blanket. The others give him great speed to go to on the outside. They do not look like a great running team. And from the films I've watched of them in preseason, they are having trouble at left guard.

Defensively, they have two outstanding backs. I think Lawyer Milloy is the best safety in the league, and Ty Law is one of the top corners. I'm happy for both of them. We had high hopes for them when we brought them into New England, and both of them have worked hard to become the kind of players they are right now.

I feel good about my team, and the way we are ready to start the season, but believe me, you never know what a team is going to do until you play that first game. So I'm a little nervous. Sunday when I get to the stadium I'll take an Inderal pill about an hour before kickoff, and another one just before the start of the game. That should control my arrhythmia, which is triggered by adrenaline, and I know I'll have more adrenaline before this game than I need.

SEPTEMBER 14, 1999

Last Saturday morning, the day before our opener with the Patriots, I was sitting in my office talking to a couple of old friends. I told them about how bad I felt for poor Dick Vermiel coaching the Rams. Dick is a good friend, and I called to console him when he lost his quarterback, Trent Green, to a knee injury in the final preseason game. He was devastated. He had built most of what he wanted to do on offense this year around Green, and now he had to go with a kid named Kurt Warner out of the World Football League. He has never started an NFL game.

I relate to guys like Vermiel, as well as Mike Ditka and Dan Reeves. They are all guys who started coaching in the 1980s, like myself. We're contemporaries. When we're not playing them, I root for them. I want them to do well, so I called Mike and Dan last week to wish them luck, too.

Reeves went to the Super Bowl last year and doesn't think his team is going to be as good. They lost Tony Martin, who was signed by Miami as a free agent, and they don't have anyone to replace him. Ditka, in one day, lost his best defensive player, Joe Johnson, for the year, and then William Roaf, one of the best offensive tackles in the league. The Saints already had their big running back, Ricky Williams, down with an ankle injury, so I was feeling sorry for Mike.

Now, though, they are all feeling sorry for me. Sunday, two days ago, I had the worst day of my life on a football field. I've

Vinny Testaverde being helped off the field in the season opener.
Not a happy sight.

never been through anything like it. I lost four starters to injury in just a matter of a few minutes, and then we blew the game at the end with some dumb mistakes and lost to New England, 30–28. We had the game won, and then we gave it back to them.

I lost my star quarterback, Vinny Testaverde, for this season with a ruptured Achilles tendon in his left leg. He didn't even get hit and the leg went on him. This guy is not only one of the best-conditioned athletes on my team, he is also one of the best I have ever been around. The injury doesn't make any sense. He had no pain or problem with that leg whatsoever, and it just tore apart on him.

Achilles tendon injuries are not unusual to quarterbacks, but this one is different. Johnny Unitas, Sonny Jurgensen, and Dan Marino are three quarterbacks who had this injury. But all of their injuries were on the right leg. Vinny's was on the left. It seems reasonable that a quarterback with this type of injury would have it happen to the right leg, because tens of thousands of times during his career, dating back to high school, he has dropped back to pass and then pushed off his right foot to make the throw. Eventually that causes a problem, and the result could be the Achilles tendon letting go. Nothing like that happened to Vinny.

We were down, 10–7, in the second quarter, driving for a touchdown in their territory, and Vinny made a handoff to Curtis Martin. Curtis was running to his left, had a big hole set up in front of him, when Willie McGinest made a hell of a play. We had him blocked when he lunged through the air and reached out as far as he could with his hand, slapped at the ball, and knocked it out of Curtis's hands. The ball rolled backward. Vinny was standing about three yards away when the ball came loose. On film, you could see him push off to take a step with his left foot, getting ready to dive for the ball. Then, in a flash, he was down on the ground grabbing his left ankle. Vinny knew he was finished right away.

My medical people tell me that when he put down his left heel, and then pushed down on his toes to lunge, a tremendous amount of stress was placed on the Achilles, which became elongated and stretched to its maximum and then just snapped.

He went to the Lenox Hill Hospital, had it repaired surgically, and he's dealing with it pretty well. I spoke with him and told him it was just a bad break, and to put it behind him. Vinny's pretty good at getting on with the future, and I know he will work his ass off to make a comeback next year.

I'm feeling bad for myself right now, but I think I'm feeling worse for him. This is a kid who has gone through a lot of adversity and tried his best, playing for some teams that weren't very good.

When he became available to us in the spring of 1998, we studied him as a coaching staff and came to the conclusion that he could really be good with us. He has a great arm. He can make all the throws. In the past, he had just been prone to making some bad decisions with the football at the most inopportune times.

The first time we talked about him possibly coming to the Jets I told him he did one thing consistently that we did NOT like, and if he corrected that, we felt he would play much better than he had been. In our study of the games he had played in Tampa, Cleveland, and Baltimore we came to the conclusion that he had a major flaw: when he was back to pass, and his primary receiver was not open, he dropped his arm down and started to run around before making the pass. This is when he threw most of his interceptions. When he stood in the pocket, had someone open, and threw on time, he had great success. We told him when he signed with us and started to practice that once he dropped his arm down with us and started to run, to keep on running. We did not want him trying to throw on the run. He did that last season and had his greatest year. In fact, he averaged 7.5 yards per rush, which is great for a quarterback when you consider that the kneel-downs at the end of a game—which we had a lot of last year with our winning record—also count against his run average.

I'll give you another interesting story of how diligent this kid is once you point him in the right direction. In each of the places he had played before he came here, the team had made up a wrist band, which held a sort of cheat sheet of their plays, for him to wear in practice and in games. The first day he came to practice he came over to me, wanting to know where his wrist-band was. I told him we didn't do that. I never did that with any of our quarterbacks. I told him if he wanted it, to do it himself. So he did. Every day during the whole season, before practice and before games, he went to a computer in our office and typed out his own wristband. He did this by himself. Coincidentally, this became a great teaching tool. By doing it himself he had to think about the plays and when we wanted them to be used in a game before typing them all out. It made him think about everything we wanted him to do. This continual mental repetition turned out to be a big plus for him and, I believe, was a major contribution to the Pro Bowl season he had.

Even though he had some pain after the surgery, he was back here in the complex. He is going to stick around and try to help out Mirer and the other quarterbacks. Mirer is the guy, and we've got Tupa and Lucas to back him up.

Let me get back to the Patriots game. We lost more than Vinnie to injury. Leon Johnson, my second best runner behind Martin, is my punt returner and a guy we count on thirty-five plays a game. He's out for the season with a severe injury. He got hurt returning a kickoff and tore two ligaments. Jason Ferguson, my best defensive lineman, has ankle and knee injuries and is out for at least a month. My tight end Eric Green has a neck injury, and I don't know when he will play. We'll find out more about Green. When I went after him in free agency, people told me I wouldn't be able to count on him. They said he was the kind of guy who won't play when he is hurt, and won't show up on the field if things don't look good. That's the situation we have right now. Things don't look good. Testaverde, Johnson, Ferguson, and Green are all starters. Chrebet and Otis Smith, both injured in preseason, are starters.

So I go into Buffalo this weekend to play the Bills without six starters, and the Bills won't be very friendly because they were beaten in Indianapolis last Sunday. People called it an upset. I didn't. I thought the Colts would knock them off, even though I think this is a good Buffalo team and a bad team for us to play in our condition. They are very sound on defense. They don't give up the big play or make the foolish mistake, like we did against New England. They can also rush the passer, so we are going to have to change our approach on offense and do what Mirer can do best.

He was in here first thing Monday morning. He'll be in here early and staying late all week. We don't have a feel for him yet and what he can do because we traded for him so late in training camp. He has to tell us what he is comfortable with, and what he cannot do. You don't want your quarterbacks trying to make plays they are not comfortable with and don't have a lot of confidence in.

As soon as Vinny was out for the year, the media started talking about getting someone from somewhere. Who? Who is out there that is better than what we have? That's why we made the trade for Mirer because we felt that he was the best that was available, and we looked all around.

Everyone thinks they know what goes on in this league, but they really don't. All the Monday morning quarterbacks. The media. These Fantasy Football guys. All experts.

The truth is, there are not enough qualified quarterbacks for the number of teams we have in this league. This is called polarization. The teams that have the best quarterbacks are the ones that are picked to be in contention for the Super Bowl at the end of the year. You don't see any teams picked as contenders without a name quarterback. And many of these guys are recycled. Guys that failed in several spots, hung around long enough, and then came back late in their careers to do well.

Look at last year's Pro Bowl quarterbacks. Doug Flutie went from the New Jersey Generals in the United States Football League to the Chicago Bears, to the Patriots, to Canada for seven years, and then to Buffalo. Randall Cunningham was out of football for a year, his career over until they recycled him in Minnesota. Chris Chandler, traded all over the place, ends up in Atlanta and takes them to the Super Bowl last year. Vinny had the same deal here.

There are so few quarterbacks capable of playing at a high level in this league that we went out and invented a bunch of them last year in the draft. Five young kids went on the first round. That never happened before. That's how desperate teams are, that they give some of these kids inflated ratings to justify making them first-round picks. The league simply does not have enough frontline quarterbacks to go around.

Mirer was the rookie of the year in Seattle but couldn't get it done there, or in Chicago, or in Green Bay. Hopefully, we can put him on the right track here, but it isn't going to be easy.

The number one thing I have to do this week, as the coach of this team, is to not let it die. The team's psyche is very fragile at the moment. Since the end of last season we were reading in the papers, and hearing from the media, how we were on our way to the Super Bowl. The day after the New England game, we were done. Finished. Cooked. Even though we have fifteen games to play, we didn't have a chance. When something like this happens, whenever you lose your quarterback, especially a Pro Bowl player, your team gets apprehensive.

After the game in the locker room at Giants Stadium, I told them not to blame the injuries. We lost the game for the same reasons most games are lost in this league. We made dumb mistakes at critical points. We had the lead, 28–27, and the ball with four minutes to go. We had good field position, and all we had to do was run out the clock. We had just run for two first downs, and this is where maybe we got a little too smart for ourselves. We did not do well all day in third and long situations, which we wanted to avoid with Mirer in the game. We also anticipated that New England would be conscious of the run on first down when they considered what the situation was. First down. We had the ball. The clock was running out. We called a pass play, and Mirer throws an interception. But it wasn't his fault. Twice on the play, the Patriots interfered with the intended receiver, Keyshawn Johnson. Not once. Twice. But the call wasn't made. The ball got tipped, it bounced around, and they picked it off for an interception. Then they moved it down the field, used up the clock, and kicked an easy field goal with three seconds left to beat us.

A year ago, one of the strengths of our defense, which was one of the best in the league, was stopping teams on third down. We beat New England twice, and that was a big part of our success. We gave Drew Bledsoe a lot of different looks in our third-down package, and we got the best of it. In this game he chewed us up on third down. He made five big third-down throws for a total of 175. That's an average of 35 yards per completion, which is unheard of in this league. We also had six penalties on offense. Three of those came when Tom Tupa was in the game as quarterback, and I attribute those to the difference in the way Vinny makes the cadence call at the line of scrimmage in comparison to Tom. Tupa had a different tempo, and our guys in the line are not used to it.

Not having Otis Smith in the game hurt us, too. I had to bring a practice squad player, Jermaine Jones, onto the active roster that morning of the game to give us some protection at corner. Against most teams we wouldn't have had to do that. But New England has a good group of wide receivers and can throw four guys at you with speed and the ability to go deep. We anticipated some fourwide receiver sets from them, and Jones would be our fourth cover guy in this situation, if it came up. In the second period it came up. We sent Jones in. He had Tony Simmons to cover.

Simmons is going to be a good receiver in this league. The Patriots took him in the draft a year ago, and he has great speed. He was the dash champion of the Big Ten in track when he was at Wisconsin. Well, Simmons ran right past our guy Jones down the sideline to catch a fifty-eight-yard touchdown pass from Bledsoe on third down.

Jones made a bad play. He should have done a much better job of covering. We were up, 7–3, at the time, and if they get an incomplete, we get the ball back. Instead they go up, 10–7. Things like that happened all day, which is why I told the team not to blame injuries. Blame the way they played.

When they came back to practice on Monday, I had to deal with them psychologically. Here's what I told them:

"All the excuses are in place if you want to use them. If you do, you will not have a productive year. If we play the way we are capable of, then we can become the most dangerous opponent in the league." I told them we were going to find a complementary way to score on offense, and had to play better defense than we did against New England. That was simply a poor effort, and we have the ability to play much better, and HAD to play much better to win.

A year ago Mark Brunell, the fine quarterback of the Jacksonville Jaguars, suffered a serious knee injury playing against the Giants in New York. The Jaguars coach Tom Coughlin coached for me on the Giants for three years, and I like Tom a lot. During our run to the Super Bowl in '90, Boston College came after Tom to be their head coach. I recommended him highly. Tom is one of the best coaches in the league. He runs his team with a firm hand, and gets the most out of what he has. We were very lucky to beat them in the playoffs last year.

Anyway, I called him the day after Brunell was injured and told him the most important speech he was ever going to give as a coach was the next one to his team. I told him not to go in there and hang his head. I told him to stand up in front of them with a positive attitude and tell them how they were going to adjust, and how they were going to win without Brunell.

The rest of the players held the fort until he got back, and they ended up winning the division and playing us in the playoffs.

We can still win, if our players think they can. It might be bumpy for a couple of weeks until we get it all squared away, but if we can stay close, we can be in the hunt at the end of the year.

The local press is making a big deal out of the turf in Giants Stadium after the injuries. Chrebet got hurt there in preseason without getting hit. Vinny went down without getting hit. Some think that Leon Johnson's knee buckled before he got hit. We don't have a good look at it on film. It just looked to me like he ran into the pile and something happened.

I've coached more than a hundred games in that stadium and never saw anything like this. I don't think it has anything to do with the artificial surface. They're talking about putting grass in Giants Stadium next year, which will be fine with me, if they can guarantee that it will have good grass for sixteen games. A bad grass field is just as dangerous as turf.

But I'll deal with that next year, if I'm here next year. That's still to be decided. I felt great last Saturday about the way things were going, and then I got reminded that this can be the most humbling of all games. You are never quite on top in the NFL until the last play is over and you are standing there holding the Lombardi Trophy. Until that happens, every play is a potential disaster.

SEPTEMBER 22, 1999

Right now I've got a fragile football team to deal with. We got beat, 14–3, in Buffalo last Sunday, and just played a bad football game when we needed to be at our best with all of the guys who are out hurt. Our confidence is starting to go. You can see it in the faces of some of our players. They expected big things to happen this year. They worked very hard in the off-season, thinking we had a real shot at the Super Bowl, and now they sense it is slipping away.

That's the thing about this game. It doesn't make any difference whether a player is young or old, a rookie or a seasoned veteran. They lose confidence when they can't get something done. Confidence comes with success. Each time you do the job, play a good game, confidence rises. Some rookies never get it, because they don't get to the point where they succeed. They can't get enough good plays behind them to gain that confidence you need to be a great player in this league. Older guys lose confidence when they can't make the plays they used to make. When a guy starts to lose it, he's the first to know it, and the last to admit it. Things become more difficult to do. Unless we put some wins together, it's going to be hard to keep what confidence we have left.

Even though they beat us without a lot of difficulty, Buffalo didn't impress me. They're a good team, not a great team. In fact, I think they were a better team a year ago than what they

Doug Flutie. We had a good record against him, but Buffalo beat us this time.

showed us Sunday night. If we played any kind of game ourselves, we would have beat them. I didn't think they were ready
to play. Still, they played better than we did.

We went into the game with a very simplistic, conservative
plan to make it as easy as we could for Mirer. We wanted to
avoid the big mistake early in the game, like turning the ball
over deep in our territory or doing something that would shake
up Mirer. No high-risk passes. The decisions he would have to
make would not be complicated, and we mixed in our normal
running game.

On defense, we handled Buffalo pretty good a year ago. For
that reason, we weren't going to change much. We beat them
twice in 1998 by getting some people in front of Doug Flutie,
and keeping him in the middle of the pocket. He is most dangerous when he starts moving around and improvising. Making
plays is what he does well. Throwing the ball with accuracy is
not one of his great strengths. Many times he will force the ball
into tough situations, and this gives a team the chance to get
some interceptions.

The guy we missed most in this game was our nose tackle,
Jason Ferguson. A year ago, when we had him on the field for
the Buffalo games, we shut down their running game. He's our
best run defender. He can dominate the guy in front of him. He's
out with leg problems, and we had to replace him with a rookie,
Jason Wiltz, and a veteran, Ernie Logan, who was coming back
from a strained muscle injury. They couldn't get the job done,
but it wasn't all their fault. The linebackers playing behind them
weren't that good either. Buffalo ran the ball down our throats.
They got over two hundred yards on the ground. And when you
control the ball, you control the game. I couldn't believe the way
they were hammering our defense. They just do not have the
kind of running game that should get 224 yards on the ground
against us. Part of this was because our offense was ineffective.
We couldn't score any points, and we held the ball for only
twenty-three minutes.

We had a shot to do something early in the game. The score was 0–0 at the end of the first quarter, which was okay with us. Mirer had his feet on the ground. We hadn't made any big mistakes, and Buffalo missed a couple of field goals. Then we got the ball and put a good drive together. We marched it all the way to their one-foot line, where I had a decision to make. Should I take the easy field goal to get points on the board, or should I go for the touchdown? Unless the score dictates otherwise, my rule of thumb in this situation is to run the ball if it is one yard or less, and kick it if we have more than a yard. We had only one foot. That's the best percentage play. When you're that close to the goal line and you want to run the ball, it's critical to beat the other team at the snap count. That's the benefit of being on offense. Your team knows when the ball is going to be snapped. The defense doesn't. You have to hit the defense quickly before they can penetrate. But we were whipped on the play. Randy Thomas, a rookie, was at right guard, and we got beat right there. They stuffed our people on the line of scrimmage, and we were stopped short.

That was a tremendous emotional lift for Buffalo and a downer for us. It would have meant a lot to get up on them 7–0 in their stadium. Instead, they turned around and drove the ball ninety-nine yards to score and go ahead 7–0 at the half. At worst, it should have been 3–0. We had a shot at Flutie in the backfield on a short yardage play and missed. If we made the tackle, they would have had to try a field goal. But they kept the drive going, and Flutie made a long run out of a scramble to set up the touchdown.

We did nothing in the second half. Buffalo took over the game on the ground. We killed ourselves on offense. In a normal NFL game, you get the ball fourteen times. In this game, we had six offensive penalties. We have research to show that when you have the ball and get an offensive penalty, your chances of scoring are cut in half. We had stupid penalties: two hands to the face, a couple of false starts, and an illegal shift. Stupid stuff, which tells me we had a lack of concentration. When you don't concentrate the way you should, you become careless and not precise. Then our receivers had six dropped passes. Put the two together, six penalties, six dropped balls, you set yourself back and don't move the ball. Three of the dropped balls were over twenty yards. That stifles you. That's why you wind up with three points instead of seventeen or twenty.

If we had any success in the passing game we would have scored. We could run the ball. We averaged close to five yards a carry. We like to run at Bruce Smith. Jumbo Elliott is bigger than he is and has success against him. Bruce's quickness makes him a great pass rusher, but he is light and not that big for a defensive end. His size limits his ability to be effective against the run, so he tries to avoid blocks by running around them. When a defensive player does that, you can run right at him.

Flutie played a pretty good game. He's great at improvising. He's got an exceptional ability to escape and be elusive. But he makes too many careless throws. At the start of the second half he threw one right to our defensive back Ray Mickens, and he dropped what should have been an interception. They took the game over in the second half and just pounded us on the ground.

I like playing in Buffalo. It's a good football city. The fans are tuned in. They know how to impact a game. A lot of cities don't get that. The fans are quite aware of when to bring up the noise level in Rich Stadium to hinder the opponent and help the home team at the same time. One of the more enjoyable games I ever coached was when we beat them last season in Buffalo to win the division. We had just beaten Miami the Sunday night before in a tough game that was up for grabs until we sacked Dan Marino late in the game. He fumbled, and we ran it in for the deciding touchdown. Then we had to go to Buffalo on a short week. Instead of the usual Sunday afternoon, the game was on Saturday. We had one less day to prepare. The stadium was electric that day and the hitting was fierce, a real slugfest. The game turned to us on three big plays. They turned the ball over twice, and Vinny threw a bomb to Dedric Ward down the sideline for a game-winning touchdown. It could have gone either way until that point.

We are now at a point where we could lose four or five in a row, and that would kill our playoff hopes. You have to win ten games in this league to get into the playoffs, and if you lose the first five, you have to win ten of the last eleven. That's just about impossible.

We have Washington coming in here Sunday. I looked at them on film this week, and they may be the best offensive team in the league right know. They scored eighty-something points in their first two games against Dallas and the Giants. They are that good on offense.

Something positive has to happen to us soon, or these players are going to stop believing. You can say you have to overcome adversity, but mentally it is difficult to overcome because until something good happens, there isn't any evidence that anything will. Every year in this league you have to prove it all over again. And until you demonstrate that you can do it year after year, no matter who you are, you wonder if you can get it done again. That's one of the great things about this game. It can be the most humbling to the best teams and the greatest players. I think if we can get to the sixth game with two wins, then we still have a shot at the playoffs. We're supposed to have three of our starters back from injury: Chrebet, Ferguson, and Otis Smith.

Denver and Atlanta, the two Super Bowl teams from last year, are in the same boat as us. Neither of them has won a game. Atlanta lost their main guy, Jamal Anderson, for the year, and their quarterback, Chris Chandler, has been hurt. I guarantee you right now that the players on that team don't feel they have a very good shot. Denver is struggling, too, with their uncertainty at quarterback. I still think Denver is good enough to overcome that, but you never know.

I've got my own problems. I still think Mirer is going to be okay. He didn't beat us in Buffalo. I'm switching to a little different strategy this week. Last week, after we lost the opening game to New England, I worked them hard. So now I'm going to back off of them physically. I took them out of pads to make the practices easier. I'm trying to put it all on the mental aspect of the game. I told the players, "I'm going to have you feeling very good for this game. You are going to have a lot of energy. We're not going to have a lot of contact. I want you ready to hit on Sunday." Last year we started off 0 and 2, so I backed off the physical stuff. The next week, we beat the Colts, 44–6, and had over three hundred yards rushing.

When you are in this situation as a coach, you have to make adjustments. Last year when we were going into New England for a critical Monday night game, I walked off the practice field three days before the game and let them practice by themselves. I was so pissed off because, as a team, their attitude was bad. I've done this several times in my career and found it to be effective. It's my way of saying to the team, "Okay, you don't want to be coached today, coach yourself." If they're not that interested, then there's no sense staying out there wasting your time. When it happens, I just leave.

This is a week-to-week thing in coaching, especially over a twenty-game season, counting the preseason. Every week has a different theme to it, and as a coach, you have to figure out which is the best way to approach it. It's just like being a jockey. I love horse racing. I own a piece of a couple of horses, and I enjoy hanging around horse people when I'm away from the team. A jockey can ride the same horse ten times in a race, and that horse isn't always the same every time out. The jockey has to sense what is happening early on and then adjust to it, if he wants to get the most out of his horse that day.

As for this Washington game, I told my coaches that they are going to take a different approach. I don't want them to be buddy-buddy with the players this week. No chitchat. Be all-business. As a staff, we have to get more intense, so I'm putting them under a lot of pressure. I have some young coaches on my staff who don't understand it any better than the players. I want to create an atmosphere of tension. This is not business as usual. It's all business and nothing else. Get the players ready to play. Be direct. Be good teachers, but don't be cordial. Don't be friendly. I don't want friendly.

Despite the problems other teams have had with him, Bryan Cox is a team leader who never makes excuses.

SEPTEMBER 30, 1999

We had a shot to beat a pretty good Washington team and we just handed the game back to them. Here it is, take it. I say pretty good because there aren't many really good teams in this league right now, which just goes to show how a few things going bad can hurt the supposed "best teams." Denver is 0 and 3. We play them next out there. That ought to be fun. Atlanta is 0 and 3. Minnesota is not as good. All of those teams are missing a few good people from a year ago, like we are, and they are not playing the way everyone thought they would before the season started.

I do know this: We had a damn good football team before the final preseason game. Then we lost Chrebet. Then we lost the rest of them in our first game. We've been going steadily downhill ever since, and if it goes another seven or eight weeks like this, I'm going to cut my throat. I mean it.

It wasn't all bad against Washington and certainly not as bad as we played against Buffalo. Washington is better on offense. Buffalo is better on defense. This was Mirer's best game. He put us in a position to win, which at this point is all we want him to do. We don't want to put the whole thing on his shoulders. He is not ready for that.

I thought we had the game won. We were up by a point, 14–13, with six minutes to play, and had the ball on their four-yard line with a chance to go ahead by eight. Then our young tight end, Blake Spence, got called for holding, and we had to settle for a field goal.

After this series, our defense played poorly and allowed Washington to score a touchdown that put them ahead for good. We gave up some big plays in the game and had three pass interference penalties, including two on the touchdown drive. All three were on the same guy: Ray Mickens. Ray doesn't usually start for us. He is what we call a nickel back, the fifth defensive back, who comes into the game when we think the other team is going to pass. Like all guys that are not starters, Ray has been telling me that he is good enough to start. I tell him that Aaron Glenn and Otis Smith are better. Then Otis broke his clavicle and I gave Ray his shot to start. His penalties were a big help to Washington in two of their scoring drives. After the game, I brought Ray into my office and told him, "It's easy to stand on the sideline and say I can do this and I can do that and I can be a starter. That's the easy thing to do. But when I put you in the game and ask you to play like a starter, you have to be accountable for the way you perform. This is when you find out if you can do it. Now some bad things have happened to you. You have to bounce back and respond. If you don't, bad things will continue to happen to you, and then you will start to think you really can't do this."

I tried to put a positive spin on what I was telling him. I didn't want to hurt him and have him lose confidence in himself. That wouldn't be good for either one of us, or the team. Ray told me that he just had a bad game and was going to do better. I don't think he's really going to give up on himself. What happened to him in the game was obvious on film. On those plays where he got the penalties, and all of them were deserved, he started to panic a little when the play took longer than he thought it would. When he started to lose contact with the receiver he was covering, he grabbed the guy. He needs to settle down and be more patient.

Offensively, we had eight penalties and two turnovers. You can't play like that and win.

We ran the ball better. Curtis had about eighty yards, and Parmalee had fifty. And Mirer played within himself. Right now he does not exude a lot of confidence, which is natural, because he hasn't been in this offense long enough to get that. But he is getting better. He has to get better.

The major difference between our team, which is losing this year, and the winning team we had last year is we do not have the firepower or the comeback power to win games. With the bunch we have now, we have to stay within range. Three points. Seven points. Less than two scores. If the other team goes up by ten, it would be very difficult for us to come back. Our margin of error has been cut down. We can't get over the hump right now because of too many errors on both sides of the ball. With Vinny and Chrebet playing, we had the firepower to overcome a lot of things, like the way our defense is playing right now.

I'm really disappointed in our defense. I thought we would play a lot better than we have. I don't understand it. I can understand our ineffective offense. We had better players available last year. This year, we've got more talent on defense than we did a year ago, but we are not playing the same way. We've changed the way we are playing defense, but that shouldn't have anything to do with it. We're using the linebackers more than we did last season, but our defensive philosophy is still the same.

I've always believed defense is the key to winning in any sport, I don't care what the sport is. Give me the best defensive team, and most of the time I'll come away winning. If you don't have a good defense, you are not going to win. It's that simple. At this point in the season, we are not getting a good pass rush from our guys up front, so we're going to have to blitz more than we have before in order to get it done. No matter who the quarterback is, you can't let him just sit back there in the pocket, not worried about getting hit.

We missed leading the league in points allowed by one point last year. We were aggressive, hustling, making plays, getting pressure on the passer, hitting people hard. This year, we've got one interception in three games, and that was by Bryan Cox in the opening game against New England. Let me say something about Cox right here. He's the best leader we have on this team. When we brought him in here a year ago, there was all kinds of talk about how he would disrupt our club because of the problems he had in Miami and Chicago. This guy has been great for us. He's gained the respect of his teammates because he is the most honest player we have. He doesn't sugarcoat anything, and he doesn't make excuses. If he doesn't do a good job, he says it's his fault and he moves on. Not all of these guys are like that. In fact, he's in the minority.

I told our defensive coaches in a meeting that our defense isn't hustling as a group the way it did a year ago. I think we have caused one fumble, and that wasn't even a good hit. Someone just reached out and slapped the ball out of Antowain Smith's arm in Buffalo. No one has really drilled the guy with the ball on the other team yet, really knocked the jock off someone and made him give up the ball. And we've only had three quarterback sacks. So we are not playing tough, and we are not getting after the quarterback, and it's hard to win when you are not doing those things.

As a result, we are not creating any field position for our offense, not setting up any easy scores. One has to complement the other. We are just very indecisive, and if this keeps up we are going to have to make some changes. The guys on the field aren't getting the job done. But not yet. This is still too early to give up on the season. We haven't as a staff, and I don't think the players have, even though their confidence is lacking.

We haven't quit, but I can see that they are having a tough time dealing with what has happened to us. When players are down mentally, they just don't have the same bounce in their step that they do when they are winning. There's not the same amount of noise and excitement around the team. When you're playing well, the players are more animated. In the locker room or the weight room, there's a lot more conversation than when you are losing, and it's at a higher pitch. Players are quiet in a losing atmosphere. There's more pressure, and they feel it. I don't want to see any happy players walking around anywhere near me when my team is losing. What's to be happy about? We're not putting all this work and effort into this thing to be happy.

I don't know what is going to happen when we get into Denver this weekend. They're not playing well. We played a little better. It might be a break that we're on the road this week. I think a team rallies together a little bit more on the road, and we need that right now. I like playing in Denver. When you go into a hostile environment like that, where the crowd's noise level is just about as high as it gets in the league, it really inspires you. If it doesn't, it's time to get out of this game. Either that, or you are dead.

I'm watching the Broncos on film, and they are struggling without Elway. They have a void at quarterback, and the teams that have beaten them so far have taken advantage of that. The strength of their team the last few years has been their running game with Terrell Davis. John Elway was not the John Elway of old, but he still had enough left to hurt you if your defense overplayed Davis. Teams this year are ganging up on Davis. They're packing the line of scrimmage, daring Denver to hurt them with the pass, and so far they haven't been able to do it. It's more than just the quarterback though. Their offensive line is not playing the way it had the previous few years. One year can make a lot of difference in this game, especially with older guys. The Denver defense is still good. But they are being tested more, because their offense is not controlling the ball on the ground like it did, and it's not scoring points like it did in the past.

Last year, I think they scored more points in the first period than any other team in the league. They would come out and get a jump offensively, take the other team out of its running game, then play good pass defense. Once they had the game in hand, they went back to running the ball, controlling the clock with Davis, and keeping the defense fresh at the same time. So like us, they have to find a way.

One more thing. Instant replay. We got the short end of it last week. In the game, at a critical point, Keyshawn Johnson caught a touchdown pass at the back of the end zone. It was good. The officials called it good. But then they decided to look at it on replay and they changed the call, so we ended up with three points instead of seven.

They should have never changed the call, and they should change the system. When they voted replay back in at the league meeting last spring, all the coaches were told that the only way the call on the field would be overturned was if replay showed with 100 percent certainty that the call on the field was in error. The official that called the play called it a touchdown. I looked at it on film and thought it was a touchdown. Other people who looked at it thought it was a touchdown. So how do they go and change it if the call is that close? Where was the 100 percent evidence that the official on the field made the wrong call?

I had never been a proponent of this current replay system because it puts too much on the coaches. The coach has to make the call for a replay, except in the last two minutes. Why should the coach have to make the call? Why should we have to be dragged into the officiating? We've got enough things to deal with during the game without becoming aides to the officials. The biggest thing I dislike about it is the possibility of losing a time-out as the penalty for asking for the replay, and the call not being changed. I hate that. The use of time-outs are a big part of a coach's clock management, which is an important responsibility. As a coach, I feel I might have the edge on some of the other coaches I go up against in this league. I don't want to give up that edge.

Here is what I would like to see happen in the future. The coaches are taken out of it completely. All of the instant replay decisions should be made by game officials and game officials only. Not league officials sitting up in the press box looking at some television monitor. Put guys up there who have made the calls before and know firsthand what it is all about. I don't want the referee running over to the sideline to look at a television set, with all of the noise and confusion that there is on the football field. Let it go up to the official in the booth. He makes the call. It starts with him, and not with any coach calling for a replay. If the game official in the box sees something he would like to look at again on replay, then he buzzes the referee on the field and tells the referee he is going to review the play. And then that guy, and that guy only, makes the call.

Back to the game in Denver. I told my players this week, and this was after long talks with the coaching staff, to concentrate on two things. First, reduce the number of penalties we have been getting. Second, get some turnovers on defense and special teams. I can't make it any simpler that that, can I?

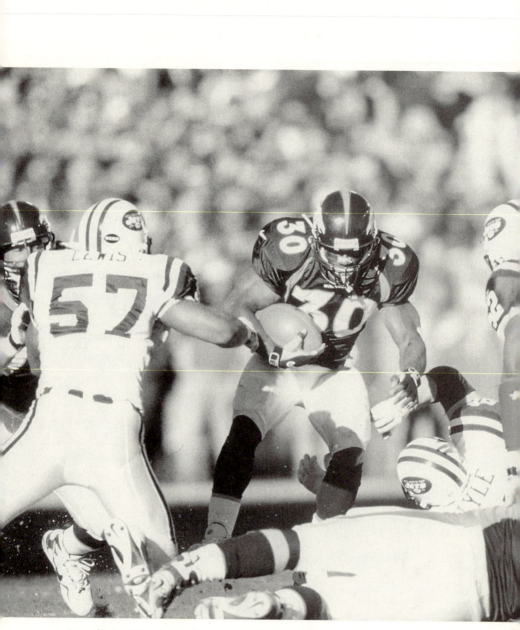

Terrell Davis is a hell of a running back. What a shame to be taken out by his own teammate.

OCTOBER 7, 1999

We finally won a game but lost two more players—Otis Smith and Chas Cascadden—who will both be out for the rest of the season. Despite that, beating Denver was a good win for us and a tough loss for them. I could see the pain in Mike Shanahan's face when we talked after the game. He just lost his best player, Terrell Davis, for the season with a knee injury. Mike knew what that meant. When you haven't won any of your first three games, and then you lose not only your best player but also one of the best players in the league, the realization hits that this is going to be a very long season with no Super Bowl at the end of it.

Mike and I have never really had a chance to get to know each other too well, but I think he is an outstanding coach. He just won two Super Bowls with a team that I didn't think was that great. They were good, but not great. If you coach in this league long enough, what is happening to Mike happens to all of us. If you stay around long enough, you have a season like he's having. Hell, I'm having another one of those seasons right now. This has been a nightmare for me.

Now the ironic thing is he is probably coaching better now than he ever has. I feel that way about myself, too. When you are losing, you coach better. When you are winning, you accept some things that have happened, even though you shouldn't have, because you won. When you lose you are on top of every detail. You scrutinize yourself, your coaches, your players, and the system you are using. Losing happens for various reasons. For both of us so far this year, the quarterback has been a big factor. Vinny got hurt for me. Elway retired for him. I've got a bunch of guys hurt. He just lost a great player.

When you are in this kind of situation, you start to hear things. "Bill should have retired last year." "He stayed a year too long." "He's lost touch with the players." It's all bull.

My first year in New England we lost ten out of the first eleven. Want to know something? I was coaching my ass off. We didn't have the talent to win. But my players tried hard every game. They wanted to win. They wanted to get better. We finished by winning four straight games and knocked Miami out of the playoffs on the final day of the season with a dramatic overtime win. When it was over, even though we had a losing season, we all felt good about ourselves because together we fought hard. I liked that team.

I didn't like my '88 Giants team even though we won ten games. When clutch time came, that team just didn't have it. I knew when that season was over we had to change if we were going to get better. I got rid of some guys and we got better. Won the Super Bowl the next year.

So far our team this year has given me a good effort, and I'm glad they got some kind of a reward against Denver. It was probably the most physical, most intense game of the season on both sides. Without Elway, Denver has lost a little of the swagger they had on offense. When John was playing, they were a cocky bunch and played with a lot of confidence. Now they are struggling to score points.

Our game plan on offense was to maintain balance at all costs. I'm still not sure about Mirer, so I'm trying not to put him into situations I don't think he can handle. We ran the ball thirty-five times. We threw the ball thirty-five times. Balance. He played his best game for us so far, but he has to improve, especially on his decision making, if we're going to take a run at getting back into the playoff picture.

We cut down on our penalties, which I had talked to the team about. We had only four on offense, compared to eight the week before. We also got six turnovers in the game, when we had only two in the previous three games. On defense, we decided to go out and hit people, and it paid off, though it took its toll.

As I mentioned at the top, Otis Smith got hurt. He broke his shoulder in training camp, then he worked his ass off to be able to come back and play. He was cleared a couple of weeks ago, but I held him out of games to be sure he was 100 percent and ready. He was in five or six serious collisions in practice during the week and came out of them fine. Then, boom, first play he tackles Davis and he fractures his clavicle in the same spot. I didn't know that at the time, because he played the rest of the half. I walked into the trainers' room at halftime and saw Otis lying there. I was surprised, so I said to the trainer: "What's wrong with him?"

The trainer said he had a broken shoulder and couldn't play anymore. Otis had played an entire half with a busted shoulder. The guy is a true warrior.

Chas Cascadden, one of my linebackers, blew out his knee and never got hit. He just twisted it running, on *grass* I might add, after all the crap I heard about the artificial turf in Giants Stadium. Believe me, it doesn't matter where you are playing and what you are playing on. If you are going to get hurt, you are going to get hurt.

Otis is thirty-three, going on thirty-four. At his age, and missing a whole season like this, I wonder about him for next year. When you get into your thirties and start to get hurt, time starts running out fast. It's the same way for Cascadden. He's been hurt three times in the last three years.

Durability is a big factor in this league. It's bigger than ever with the salary cap factor. If a player gets hurt and he can't play, you don't get any breaks with the salary cap. It's not like you can shop around and get another guy. I like both of these guys and I feel sorry for them. But I have to carry on in this business. It's sad the way things go.

When a player is hurt, it's like he is not a part of the team anymore. He comes to our facility, but he works on rehab all the time, so he won't be on the field or in meetings. It's like he's not even here. You talk to injured players from time to time, but it's mostly, how are you doing? It's the same way with their team-mates. Coaches and players that aren't hurt have to get back to business and don't have a lot of time to spend with them.

Offensively, we should have done more in Denver, especially with our defense getting six turnovers for us. But for one reason or another, we didn't score as many points as we should have. Right now my tight end position is killing our offense. Eric Green just stinks. He has stunk up the joint since the start of the regular season, and our other two tight ends, Fred Baxter and Blake Spence, have been hurt from time to time. Here is what is happening to Green: he can't run anymore. Anyone can cover him. As a result, we can't throw him the ball because he's never open. And because he's not getting the ball, he's pouting.

When he first came here, he blocked like we thought he could. One of the reasons we picked him up in free agency is because one of my linebackers, Mo Lewis, told me Green is the best blocking tight end in the business. Mo might be our best player, and if he's telling me how great Green is, I'm going to lis-ten. Same with Vinny, who played with him in Baltimore. And Pat Hodgson, my tight ends coach, coached him in Pittsburgh when he was having his most productive years. But, and I men-tioned this before, some other people warned me about this guy, that if the going got tough, he might bail out. And it looks like that is happening. His blocking has fallen off. His effectiveness is going downhill. I won't take it much longer. If he keeps on play-ing like this, his ass will be out of here. I've had my coaches talk-ing to him, trying to get him going again. We'll see what hap-pens. I've been staying away from him because I'm afraid if I go talk to him, and I don't hear what I want to hear, he won't be around here at all.

Now I'm starting to hear that we should have kept Kyle Brady, and the way things are going, maybe that is right. We wanted to keep Brady. We offered him what we thought was a hell of a contract, and what he was worth to us, but Jacksonville offered him like $800,000 more for five years. Brady was a good player for us. Not great. But he played all the time and was durable. He was not a big part of the passing game, and he didn't block well when he was standing still. That's why we used him in motion a lot—he was at his best when he was on the move. While getting ready for this Jacksonville game I noticed that they are doing the same thing with him. Moving him around.

We've got Jacksonville at home Monday night, and we have to play a lot better than we have been playing. They've really improved themselves on defense, so we need Mirer to step up more in this one. We have to try to win low-scoring games. There's no way we can open up our offense right now. We just don't have the weapons to do it. Denver was our best game on defense, but don't forget, Davis got hurt. What a fluke. Victor Green had intercepted a pass and was running it back when Davis and one of his linemen went over to make the tackle. The lineman hit Davis from behind and Davis had his foot planted in the ground. That was it. You can see his knee cave in on the films. Here's a guy that carried the ball hundreds of times without getting a major injury, and he gets taken out by someone on his own team.

We need our defense to continue to get better. Before the Denver game, we were ranked last in the league. We've been too helter-skelter in what we have been trying to do. I talked with my defensive coaching staff about it. I've got three guys who have been with me for years: Bill Belichick, Al Groh, Romeo Crennel. They are all good. I'm lucky to have them. But every once in a while, they get too schematic for my taste. Belichick and Groh are very analytical. They are always examining things, breaking them down, and coming up with new stuff. Over the years they've done a good job of it, and won a lot of ball games with the defensive plans they have put together.

Belichick will be the next head coach here unless the next owner decides to do something different. There was a lot of unfounded speculation going on about Bill after last year. He was not offered any head coaching jobs. I know, because they would have had to call me to get permission to talk to him, and no one did that. I spoke with Bill about it at the time, and he said he wasn't interested. When Mr. Hess heard some of this talk, he gave Belichick a $1 million bonus for staying. The year before though, Mr. Hess was upset about Bill talking to some other teams about a head coaching job. He told me that if he ever did it again, to let him go. But that never happened.

There was also some speculation about Romeo Crennel, our line coach. When Chris Palmer got the head job in Cleveland he asked me about Romeo. I told him I would appreciate it if he didn't look at any of the coaches on my staff. I wanted to keep them. Chris never asked permission to speak with any of them, including Romeo. The story went around that I prevented Romeo from going to Cleveland. That's not true. If he wanted to go, all he had to do was ask me and I would have let him go.

Same thing with Al Groh. George Seifert called when he got the Carolina job and inquired about Al. I had a supervisory tag on Al, which teams are allowed to place on assistant coaches in this league to prevent them from making a lateral move, going someplace else for the same title. If Al wanted to go to Carolina, I would have let him go.

But Al and Romeo would be better off staying here. They might be thinking otherwise right now. I'm laughing when I say that. These coaches are like anyone else. They like attention. They want the security of a long-term contract. But, when job opportunities come up, they also want to be able to look at those. You can't have it both ways. Either you take the long-term deal where you are, either a two- or three-year deal, or take it one year at a time, and look around without any problem.

It is important to have a cohesive coaching staff. If there is a problem on my staff, say like a couple of them aren't getting along, then I get rid of one of them. One time I had a coach who butted heads with another coach, who eventually left for a different team. Then he had a problem with the replacement I brought in, who then left. I went to the coach and said, "If you have a problem with the next guy I bring in to work with you, then you'll be gone, not him." When you take a new job and start to build your staff, you go mostly by recommendations from friends and coaches you respect. Sometimes you make mistakes. There have been a couple of instances where I let someone go after a year or two because I knew he just wasn't going to work out. You can also have trouble with coaches once your team has enjoyed some success. Some of them get a little full of themselves and think they're the reason for all the success. But they're not alone—the same thing happens with players.

I think success has hurt Jacksonville's staff. Tom Coughlin lost both of his coordinators. On offense, Palmer went to Cleveland. Defensive coordinator Dick Jauron went to Chicago. Tom brought in Dom Capers, who is very good. He's put in his own defensive scheme, which was so successful in Pittsburgh and then Carolina. Offensively, Tom has been doing a lot of it himself, and that hurts when you are trying to coach an entire ball club. Just having to be in all of the offensive meetings takes away from the other things a head coach has to do. Sometimes too much on your plate can wear you down before the season is over.

This season is wearing on me, but I'm taking it like a personal challenge. I'm trying to stay on top of the most minute things that I think can make a difference, scrutinizing everything we are doing. Our margin of error is very narrow with this team. It is tough to try to coach or manage a game when you know your team is so fragile, that one or two mistakes are just too many to overcome.

Personally, I'm doing okay. I didn't get a lot of sleep this week. But I've remedied some of that by getting this reclining chair for my office, and once in a while I grab a nap. I tell my secretary to hold all calls, and I go to sleep for about twenty minutes and wake up refreshed.

*Tom Coughlin was on my staff with the Giants and now heads the
Jacksonville Jaguars.*

OCTOBER 15, 1999

I have to make a decision about my quarterback in the next
forty-eight hours, and I'm not sure which way to go yet. Mirer
went backward in our game last Monday night against
Jacksonville, when we got beat again, 16–7. That was probably
the worst offensive performance I've ever been associated with
in the NFL. In short, we stunk.

Mirer was bad, but he had a lot of help in that department.
Almost every player we had on offense, except a couple of linemen, chipped in five bad plays each during the game, and when
that happens you are not going to score any points. Our linemen
were missing blocks, many of them in critical situations. Our
receivers were running bad routes and dropping passes. We
never established a running game. In the entire game we probably had six or seven decent offensive plays. Just six or seven.
The rest all had some kind of screwup. Mirer didn't play as well
as he did the previous two games, and I think our team is starting to lose some confidence in him, and he's losing some in himself. Mirer had a couple of good plays against Denver, but outside of that, he hasn't done much. His rating isn't good. He has
been very average. And we've tried to be very conservative to
help him out. We completed four of five passes on third-down
situations, but they were short and we didn't get the first down.
The receivers are catching the ball short of the first-down

marker, and they're also running short routes, which they will do if they are not confident about the passer.

As for the game, it was held on a windy night. I told our team in the locker room just before we went out to start the game that the wind was going to be a definite factor. I could see that in warm-ups. I've coached so many games in Giants Stadium, which can be a treacherous place to play in the wind if you don't handle it properly, that I know when the wind is going to be a major factor. So I brought the team together just before we went out on the field and told them, "When we are going into the wind, we are going to play conservative. We won't take any chances. We don't want to turn the ball over." I told them when we had the wind at our backs, we would be more aggressive.

I particularly told our punt return team to be careful because of the wind. When Jacksonville punts into the wind, I told them, keep away from the ball. The last thing I wanted to see was the ball bounce off one of our blockers and Jacksonville get it back again. If Jacksonville punts with the wind, do not let the ball hit the ground. Catch it on the fly. I've seen too many punts hit the ground with a wind like that and take off.

I had it happen to me in a big game against the Eagles. We had Philly backed up late in the game and Randall Cunningham punted a ball that our guy didn't catch and it went something like ninety yards. We never could come back from that, and we lost the game. I didn't want to see a repeat of that in this game, but it didn't take long to see it, which is typical of the way our season has been going. The first time they punted with the wind, our returner, Corey Fuller, let it bounce and it ended up going eighty-three yards. I guess I didn't emphasize it enough. I thought I did, but obviously not everyone was listening.

Our defense played an adequate game. We held Jacksonville to thirteen points, but let me say right now, that Jacksonville is not as strong offensively this year. Mark Brunell just doesn't look as sharp to me. Their best running back, Taylor, didn't play. The kid had a great rookie year and looked like he was going to be a big-time player, but he's been out hurt most of the year.

There are only a dozen weeks to go here, and he still hasn't played much. Without him they don't have a lot of speed on offense. Jimmy Smith is an excellent wide receiver with a lot of speed, but we doubled him and pretty much took him out of the game. They had a real good pass-catching tight end, Pete Mitchell, but he signed with the Giants in free agency. They miss him. He's a guy that Brunell was very comfortable throwing to, and making some key plays in a game. They picked up my tight end from last season, Kyle Brady, who is a better blocker than Mitchell but not nearly the threat in the passing game.

Jacksonville's defense is much better than it has ever been. They've upgraded it with a few new players. I see this as a "window of opportunity" season for them. Brunell and the receivers have been together a few years now, and when you depend on a pass-catch combination to score, you only have a few years to get it down. The receivers start to run down and don't play for a long time.

The way our defense played, we should have won the game. But our offense was so poor we couldn't do it. We turned the ball over twice. We couldn't convert on third down. We were still in it late in the game, behind just 13–6, and had a fourth and one deep in our own end. I decided to go for it. We still had a chance. But tight end Blake Spence missed his block, and we were stopped short. That gave them their last field goal.

We are at a point now where this team's confidence in its ability to do anything is tentative at best. Our quarterback is in a tenuous situation.

I've given our backup, Ray Lucas, a lot of snaps in practice this week, and I'm thinking about starting him this week against Indianapolis. I haven't told him that, or the media, or anyone else, because I haven't made up my mind for sure. But I'm leaning that way. The Colts have a very good offense. They've been scoring thirty points on just about everyone. I think we can do better than that, but we have to score more points than we have been scoring to give us a chance to win this game. I think we will need at least twenty points, and I don't know if Mirer can get them for us.

I think the team might respond to Lucas better. He's very competitive. The more I watched Lucas in practice this week, the better I liked him. I'm not going to say anything to anyone about it because if I do, this place will become a circus with the media running all over the place asking everyone for their comments. They'd talk to Mirer about being benched. The kid about starting. The other players about what they thought, and what it would result in, and about the quarterback position, instead of everyone focusing on beating Indianapolis.

What is happening to this team, losing the way we have, involves more than one position. We are all part of it. I told my team at the start of the week that we can't have a club fighter mentality.

In the old days of boxing you'd find a club fighter, a guy who was pretty good but knew he was never going to be a champion. He kept on fighting because it was a way to make a living. He had to keep on fighting hard, even though he never aspired to be a champion. I told them we can't have that mentality and be successful. We want to be good enough to be on top of the card at Madison Square Garden. We could not trap ourselves into thinking about going through the motions the rest of the way. If you let some of them do it, they would. It's human nature in a situation like this.

Some people are starting to point at our offensive line, because it was supposed to be the weak link before our season started, but actually it hasn't played that bad. One of the reasons it has given up some sacks is because Mirer doesn't get rid of the ball when he is supposed to. There are times he drops back to throw, and when he doesn't see anything, he starts to scramble out of trouble, which is fine with us. Then he stops, looking to throw again, and gets hit. We told him to throw the ball away. Don't take the loss. It is frustrating. There were six or seven times when Brunell was in the same situation and he just threw the ball away. This offensive line is better than the one we had a year ago. I know I can't prove it right now, but I know it is.

I just watched the Patriots–Kansas City game on film. Bledsoe got knocked all over the place. The Chiefs were putting him on the ground all day, because they knew if New England has to move the ball, it has to throw it to make yardage. I saw the same thing in the Miami-Colts game. Jesus, they must have knocked Marino down fifteen times. Fifteen.

This is not good for our game. We don't have enough good quarterbacks in this league to go around. Close to half the teams in this league—I'd say thirteen or fourteen—have quarterbacks starting for them right now who they don't like. I know that because there were three teams that called me when Testaverde got hurt and wanted to trade me their starter. I won't mention the teams because I've given them my word that I wouldn't. I'm getting crucified here in the media for not having a backup. That's fine. But half the league doesn't even have a starting quarterback they are happy with. The position of quarterback is really diluted in this league. I talked earlier about the return of guys like Testaverde, Cunningham, and Flutie, "caretaker quarterbacks" who came back last year from really nowhere to have great seasons. The talent pool at that position in college has been poor.

In fact there's only one kid in the last four or five years who came out as a quarterback who has impressed me, and that is Peyton Manning. What kills me is that we came close to getting him, and I would have taken him in a second if we had the chance. My first year with the Jets we had the first-draft choice, and Manning was thinking about leaving Tennessee early. Or at least that's what his agent said. I don't think he really was, and in the end, he stayed there and had a great season. If he had come out, we would have drafted him.

Who are the next great ones? We had five taken in the first round last year, and to be honest, I think some of those guys were invented by teams that needed to fill that position. We'll see what happens to this group over the next couple of years. None of them have made a big impression yet. I think all of them are struggling. Colleges have not been turning out talented passing quarterbacks. I think they are placing too much emphasis on the run, or guys throwing on the run, which is not conducive to what we do in this league. The desperation to find a quarterback who can really play is at an all-time high. After San Francisco saw what Flutie did for Buffalo, they went up to grab this kid named Garcia for their club. St. Louis went into the Arena League and apparently has found a great prospect in Kurt Warner, who is burning up the league.

But you are really lucky when you come up with a guy like that. They're killing me for trading Glenn Foley to Seattle during the off-season. I've seen Foley as a starter. We couldn't win any games with Foley as a starter. He started seven or eight games for the Jets and couldn't win any of them. I think he's a good fireman, a relief guy who could come in and play a half and rally your team. He's a good kid. Well liked. But to me he was never going to be a good starter.

First, he got hurt too much. In this league, if you want to compete, your quarterback has to be durable.

Second, when the other teams found out he couldn't throw the ball, he started to have problems. I've had other players like this. Jeff Rutledge played for me with the Giants as a backup. He was a brilliant guy who played at Alabama in a highly competitive program that was honed to win. But he was limited, and there were certain throws he just couldn't make. Once he got some playing time, the other teams figured out what those limitations were and used them against us. He was a great anticipator, though. He would stand on the sideline without any practice reps during the week and, if he had to play, still execute the timing of the game efficiently. Jeff understood what his assets and liabilities were, and he got the most out of what he had.

There are not many quarterbacks in this league who can make all the throws, who can get the ball to any spot on the field with a lot of speed behind the pass. Some guys don't have the arm strength to throw the deep fade, or the deep sideline. And when teams realize, for example, that a passer cannot hurt them deep, then they will jump all over his shorter routes and take them away from him. Then he has nowhere to go with the ball, and you as a coach have a major problem.

Flutie is a guy who might be the best example of how to overcome limitations. Because of his height, he has a hard time making throws over the middle. He doesn't see the field that well with the taller offensive linemen in front of him, so he adjusts and improvises to make plays. He takes his game to the perimeter of the field, outside of the tackles, and creates. He's wonderful at it. He'll run around until he sees everything clearly downfield and then make his throw. He has tremendous quickness and is very elusive. But there is only one of him.

Right now we don't have a healthy, proven quarterback, so we are in trouble. Same with Dan Reeves in Atlanta. He can't keep his guy on the field. Ditka doesn't have a top quarterback in New Orleans. Before the season everyone picked Arizona to do big things because of what they did last year. Now this Jake Plummer kid is really struggling and they are not winning. They have to wonder if he's as good as they thought he was going to be. The Giants don't have one. They're playing two guys, in and out, but not scoring any points. Philadelphia is trying to develop one, but they are not in good shape for this season. The Packers have won four games, but if it wasn't for Brett Favre saving their ass, they would have lost all four of them.

It is hard to find a quarterback that has it all: the combination of skill, toughness, and intelligence. Beyond the physical ability, they need to be adept at leadership, which entails knowing how to manage the game by making the right decisions, avoiding bad plays and sometimes turning bad plays into good ones and being elusive. Elusiveness helps a lot. This doesn't mean a guy has to be a runner. Some guys—Marino and Elway were really good at this—make pass rushers miss by sliding a step one way or the other and avoiding the tackle to make a throw.

The thing I loved about Phil Simms, my Giants starting quarterback, is that he never made an excuse. If something went wrong, he took it on his own shoulders. It was always his fault.

Even if the receiver did something wrong, Phil would say: "Hey, I'll get it to you. Try to deepen that route up a little bit." Or, "I was late with the throw"—even if he knew he was on time with the throw. He would make everyone around him feel that they were doing well and he was the one who was holding them back. Phil was tough. Phil was fiery. And his teammates respected him for that.

Jeff Hostetler was our third quarterback at the time, and he moved up to second when Rutledge left. Hostetler was very bright. He was a play-action passer coming out of college at West Virginia. His passing mechanics needed improvement, though. He threw the ball with a very low trajectory. He kept his elbow down, which is not good if you want to throw the ball properly. But he made up for this with his terrific athletic ability. He knew how to run. He was elusive. He could create and improvise. When Simms got hurt late in the year in 1990, Hostetler won three playoff games for us and the Super Bowl. After that, he left us and went to the Raiders, where he never found the same success. He didn't have the cast around him in Oakland that he had in New York.

My first year in New England we picked up a guy named Scott Secules from Miami. He was a backup there with Marino. He didn't get to play much. We were drafting Bledsoe, and I wanted to bring in a veteran guy who might be able to show Bledsoe how to prepare for a game, and play some until Drew was ready. I also picked up Secules because he could run a little bit. We had a terrible team, so Secules made some plays by scrambling around. With Secules, we did not have to throw Bledsoe to the wolves.

Drew was just twenty years old. He was young and immature. He came out of a passing offense in Washington State, so we tried to teach him the first year how to become a play-action passer. We didn't have the line or the backs to run the ball, but we still ran it. Scott Zolak was also on that team, but in those days, Scott was like Drew—a kid with a strong arm but not much experience.

Drew started to come along the second half of his rookie year.

We won four in a row at the end. The next year was a big surprise. We made the playoffs when no one picked us to be even close. We won the final seven games of the regular season and had to win in Chicago on the last week to make it as a wild card. Drew really played well.

His third year we had some problems. A lot was expected because we made the playoffs the year before, but things didn't work out. Early in the year, Drew got hit and hurt in a game in San Francisco. He separated his left shoulder. The doctors took him to the dressing room, and when they returned, they said Bledsoe could play. I put him back in. He got knocked around and we lost. I took a lot of heat for it. The media tried to paint the picture that I did it to show up Drew and that I didn't like him. That's not true at all. If our medical people had said he couldn't play that day in San Francisco, I would not have put him back in the game.

Like any young guy, Drew made some mistakes. But he learned from those, and now he is one of the top quarterbacks in the game. He has experienced the things you have to experience in this league to get to the top level. You have to go through the tough times and do things you don't want to do until they don't bother you anymore, and this is what he has done.

When I came here to the Jets, Neil O'Donnell was the quarterback and Foley was his backup. O'Donnell was kind of a reticent guy who was quite withdrawn. You never knew what he was thinking. He can win some games for you if he plays in a controlled system and has a good cast around him, but he's not the kind of guy that can carry a team. I got rid of him because I didn't think we could ever have been better than 8 and 8, or 9 and 7, with him, and that's not good enough to go where I want to go. I took him out of a couple of games that first year, put Foley in, and we rallied back to win. Neil didn't like being taken out.

Testaverde is different. He is totally accountable. He's never made an excuse for anything. He is able to put the last play away and get on to the next one. He's been sitting in the press box watching the games. Then we talk a little bit the next week.

After the last game I asked him what he saw. He said, "There were five or six plays we should have known where to go pre-snap and we didn't." It's stuff like that, the ability to know what you're going to do before you even snap the ball, that makes it a shame we don't have Vinny now. If we did, this whole thing would be different.

The way Vinny is rehabbing he could probably play in December, but we can't bring him back because we put him on the injured reserve list, which means he can't play the rest of the season. I think the league should change this rule. We should be able to bring players back off injured reserve when they are healthy again. There are just no quality players available to replace starters when they're injured.

Figure it out. There are thirty-one teams in the league, soon to be thirty-two when Houston gets its franchise. There are fifty-something players on each team. The talent pool available out there is nonexistent. There is no one left to go after once you get an injury during the season. We put in the injured reserve rule years ago, before we had this present collective bargaining agreement and the salary cap restraints that go with it.

Before that, teams were stashing players. If they had some good young players who might help them in the future, rather than cutting them or waiving them in training camp, they'd say the player was injured and "stash" him. They'd give the player a phony injury and keep him around practicing with the team to prevent him from going to another team. It was illegal. But there were a lot of teams in the league that did it. Washington was the worst. We used to kid in the league that the Redskins were paying more players that were stashed than were on the regular roster.

But it's not possible to stash anymore. The salary cap took care of that. The economics of the league prohibit it. You don't have enough money to pay a sixty- or seventy-man roster. I would be a strong advocate of what could be called: "Moves from Injured Reserve." You would have a certain number of moves each season to bring players back from injured reserve . Maybe just two or three moves. Take New England. They had Ted Johnson, an excellent linebacker, get hurt in preseason. They knew he had a chance to get back, so they couldn't put him on injured reserve. They had to keep him on their roster and play a man short. We put Vinny on the list, so we can't get him back, even when he is ready to play. As a result, we can't put our best product on the field. And that's not right.

The second thing I think we need to consider is allowing trades during the season. Such trades are almost nonexistent, again because of our salary cap rules. There is no way to trade one player for another once the season starts because of the economics. The reason for this is: when a player is traded, the money he has coming to him stays with the team that traded him, and counts on their cap.

When a player signs a bonus in this league, he gets the money up front, but in the accounting department, his bonus is spread out over the length of his contract. If a player gets a $10 million bonus in a five-year contract, it is prorated on the books, at $2 million a year. However, if they trade him, what he has left on the books in bonuses comes forward immediately. I think the league has to consider having a provision where if there's no economic advantage created, teams would be allowed to make a trade. For example, let's say I've got a player making $500,000 this year and the team I want to trade with has a player making the same amount. Let's make the trade. Forget about accelerating whatever bonus money there is coming to either player, and make the trade for an equal salaried player. If I'm around here next year, I'm going to push for both of these changes.

Peyton Manning is the best quarterback to come out of college in the past five years.

OCTOBER 18, 1999

It's a little bit after 7:00 in the morning, and I'm tired and miserable. We lost another game that we probably should have won, and I have to point the finger at myself on this one. We lost to the Colts on a field goal at the end and right before that I made a decision that hurt our chances, and probably cost us the ball game. When the game was over I told the team I was sorry for what happened, and that I couldn't get them over the hump. I told them the same thing at the team meeting Monday.

I wish I could describe in detail what I feel like right now. It's just three or four days of absolute sick-to-your-stomach misery. When I'm like this, I have to be careful when I talk to the media. They try to antagonize me.

I talked to Dan Reeves a little bit. He's going through the same thing, except his team just got beat, 41–10. No matter how long you have coached, no matter how many games you have won, no matter how many playoff games, conference championships, Super Bowls, it doesn't matter. You are not winning now, and that is what counts. You think you suck. You think you are a loser as a coach. That's the way I feel. I'm miserable to everyone: to my coaches, to my players, to the people who work here in the building. I don't mean to be that way. I try to be respectful. You try to be human, but you are just miserable.

All of this losing just feeds the uncertainty around here. The people are reading from time to time about a new owner coming in. The process is in motion, and every once in a while there's another story about it in the news. Then people start asking more questions. When the new owner gets in here the record isn't going to be that good, so I don't know if he will want me back, and right now I haven't made any decision about coming back. The other coaches are already beginning to worry about their futures. I can sense it. Who are we? Who's the next owner? What's he going to think when he walks in here?

I'm trying different things to get us another win and shake us out of this losing streak, which is where Ray Lucas came in. He gave us the lift we hoped for, taking us down the field and scoring some points on the first three of four possessions. But we gave the game back at the end. The score was tied at 13. There were about four minutes left. We had just driven the ball on the ground with Curtis Martin to their three-yard line.

I decided to call a play-action pass. I should mention that people are starting to make a big deal out of me calling the plays, like it's something new. Let me point out that our entire offensive coaching staff sets the plan. We all work on it together. We decide as a unit what we are going to do, down and distance, situation to situation, at every point in the game. It's just on Sundays, I will make the final call. I did it a lot in New England. I'm doing more of it here. Quite frankly, when Vinny went out, I knew it wasn't going to be great. I need to play every game a certain way, the way I think this team has to play in order to win without Vinny. I knew we were going to struggle on offense, and there was going to be a lot of heat. I decided to take the heat. Not my coaches.

The same kind of thing is happening in Minnesota. They were great on offense last year, and Brian Billick, their offensive coordinator, left to take the head coaching job in Baltimore. They haven't played well this year. There's a lot of controversy about the play calling. The players are getting into it in the media. The coaches are talking about benching Cunningham after the great season he had a year ago. The offensive coordinator, Ray Sherman, is new and under a lot of pressure. I didn't want this to happen to my coaches. If there's anyone that's going to take a lot of crap, it should be me.

Let's get back to the play-action I called. Ray made a bad decision on the play and threw an interception that they ran back to set up the winning field goal. I made my own bad decision putting Ray in that position to begin with. Even though I think it was the right call, I'm second-guessing myself—maybe I should have played it more conservatively. Run the ball three times, hoped we got a touchdown, and if we didn't, kick a field goal with a couple of minutes left and hope we could hold on. You know, there's no guarantee you can hold on, but our defense has been playing very well the last three or four games.

This Manning kid is a dangerous player, though, and he's the best young quarterback to come into the league since Bledsoe. If he doesn't get hurt, and they put a decent cast around him, he's the kind of kid, mentally and physically, who can have a Hall of Fame career.

Let me tell you why I went for the play-action pass. The Colts were playing the run very hard. We hadn't had any luck against them in short-yardage situations in the game. They had stopped us every time. And we had been piss poor all year in goal line situations trying to run the ball in. I thought we had them set up for the play call. San Francisco runs this play a lot with Jerry Rice. We brought Keyshawn across in motion, and we tried to beat the cornerback in the flat. This is a tough play for the corner to cover. He has to run behind the line of scrimmage, where there's some traffic with his own linebackers. The quarterback in this situation is supposed to throw a fade, a high lob into the corner so nothing bad can happen to us. Either it's over the shoulder to Keyshawn for a touchdown, or out of the end zone for an incomplete pass. Either way, we shouldn't get hurt.

But Ray threw the ball flat. On a line. And the corner stepped in front of Keyshawn to make the interception.

We then had three chances to stop the Colts on third downs to send the game into overtime, but we couldn't get it done.

I'd been through this before with Ray. My first year with the Jets, we played the final game of the season in Detroit. If we won, we were in the playoffs. If we lost, we were out. Late in the game we had the lead, going down the field for a score that probably would have won the game for us. All week long we told Ray in practice, the only pass we want you to throw when you are in there is a fade. If the fade isn't there, throw the ball away. Don't force the ball. Well, we called for a fade and he decided to throw the ball to the tight end. Something we told him not to do. But he did it and Detroit intercepted. We lost the game.

Fans and the media don't understand that no matter how close you get to some players, and how much you think you know about how they will respond to pressure, you just never know.

Ray improvised some good plays, like he can do and didn't play too badly for his first time out. But these are the kind of plays that keep you from having a long pro career. Too many of those, and you don't stay around too long. But shit happens. And we have another heartbreaking loss for everyone.

Defensively and on special teams, we have been playing well. If we had any kind of consistent offense at all, we'd be in great shape. Our guys are still playing hard. I see no sign of quit in them, but this was the kind of loss that could break team spirit.

Unfortunately, Lucas got hurt and won't be able to play for a couple of weeks. Mirer, who was disappointed that he didn't start, is going to have to start again. Mirer didn't say much, but the press writes that our relationship is strained. I don't see any of that. I explained to him before the Colts game that I was looking for a spark with Ray.

Now we'll see what Rick can do. His job is to get ready to play. I don't care about what starting Ray might have done to Mirer psychologically. In pro football you are getting paid to be ready and to perform, no matter what the circumstances are.

It reminds me of what happened in Buffalo a couple of years ago. The Bills had to put Billy Joe Hobert in the game at quarterback. He didn't do the job. They lost. When it was all over, he said he didn't get ready to play because he didn't think he was going to play. Marv Levy cut him the next day, and I agree with what he did. If you are not ready to play, you don't deserve any slack.

I do have the temptation to try Tupa at quarterback, but if I do that I'll be taking a guy who is performing the best of anyone on this team at his position and putting him on the spot. I'm not ready to do it. We'll go with Mirer again. I'm bringing a couple of quarterbacks in off the street to give them a look in practice in case Ray is going to be out longer than I think. We might need some protection there.

People are suggesting that we try to get Mark Rypien or Jeff Hostetler, guys who are older, have had some success but have been out of football for a couple of years. I have a great deal of respect for what both those guys have done, but I think their day has passed. When I saw both of them play some of their final games, they weren't playing very well.

Besides the games, we've got another situation going on. We've got a nice kid named Kevin Williams on our team who is very sick and came close to dying last week. He has a very serious strep infection in his throat, and our doctors have been very concerned.

When we went out to Denver a couple of weeks ago, Kevin complained of a sore throat. Our doctors checked him out before the game and he seemed to be okay. They gave him some antibiotics. On Monday after the game, his throat was still sore, so they gave him some more. They were treating it very aggressively, but apparently the antibiotics weren't slowing it down, so they put him in the hospital. I'd say we had ten different doctors, many of them specialists for this kind of problem, looking at him and trying to treat him. But Kevin got worse. His lungs became infected and had to be drained. It became a life-and-death situation. Now he is in intensive care and seems to be stabilized.

Now we have to start reading and hearing statements from his agent, Jerome Stanley—the same guy who represents Keyshawn Johnson. I think the guy is a jerk. He is out there saying we are not taking care of Kevin, not communicating with his family, not doing what we should for him.

We are doing everything we could possibly do for Kevin and more. When it first happened, our doctors told us they would handle it and they didn't want Kevin bothered by us while he was in intensive care. They would communicate with him and his family. If it wasn't for them, I don't think he would have made it.

Stanley started mouthing off because we put Kevin on the non-football injury list. Now when we do this, we don't have to pay him a cent. A sore throat is not a football injury. Still, we kept him on the roster for two more weeks when we knew he couldn't play. He was in the hospital. That two weeks gave him enough weeks this season to give him another year toward free agency. We didn't have to do that, but we did. Second, we didn't have to pay him a cent the rest of the year. Yet we gave him two full paychecks for those two games he missed, even though he wouldn't play, and we are going to pay him half of his salary the rest of the year.

Stanley's now claiming it's a football illness. A sore throat is a football injury? A strep throat is a football injury? That is ridiculous. Let me say this about Stanley. I don't care if he's Keyshawn's agent, I'll never talk to that son of a bitch again.

NOVEMBER 3, 1999

About ten days ago, I was sitting here in the office feeling sorry for myself after another terrible loss, this one in Oakland, when I got a call. There was a report that Payne Stewart, a friend of mine, was believed to be on a plane that was out of control and would probably crash.

I met Payne through Robert Fraley. Fraley was my agent, but to me he was more of a friend. Robert was with me for seventeen years, always there when I needed him. When I was told about Payne being in trouble, I didn't think of Robert at first. Then someone else told me the reports on television said there were five people on the plane. It turned out to be six. I switched on the TV and started to watch the news broadcasts.

Then I had the horrible thought that Robert might be on the plane. I called his office at Leader Enterprises in Orlando, and one of his associates told me he was on the plane along with Van Ardan from his office, who I was also friendly with. I sat in shock, and I don't shock easily, waiting to see what was going to happen. Then I heard the news that the plane had crashed in Aberdeen, South Dakota, and everyone was dead.

Robert was certainly one of my top five friends. It was through him that I met not only Payne and Van Ardan, but also his other clients like Orel Hershiser, the late Jerome Browne, and Paul Azinger. We had a chance to spend some time together through our mutual relationship with Robert.

Robert Fraley represented both me and Dan Reeves, among other prominent NFL coaches. Losing a friend like Robert was difficult for both of us.

I was an assistant coach with the Giants under Ray Perkins when Ray left to take the head coach job at Alabama after Bear Bryant retired. He recommended me to succeed him, and our general manager, George Young, approached me about it after talking with Wellington Mara. George didn't want to negotiate with an agent. That made it tough on Robert, but he persevered, and from that point on he went on to represent some of the top coaches in the game over the years—Dan Reeves, Joe Gibbs, Tom Coughlin, Bill Cowher, Buddy Ryan, just to name a few.

I haven't told too many people this story, but Robert probably saved my career early on. In 1983, I was having a very difficult year personally. Within the space of months, both my mother and father died, and that was a lot to deal with. On top of that, my team wasn't playing very well. Toward the end of the year, I got a call from Robert, and he said that the Giants were thinking about getting rid of me. I couldn't believe it. I had the job just one year. But he said he knew for sure, because George Young had called Howard Schnellenberger and asked Howard if he was interested in the job. What George Young didn't know was that Robert also represented Howard.

George Young and Howard knew each other from their connection to Don Shula. Young started out as a scout when Shula was coaching the Baltimore Colts. When Shula went to Miami, Young went with him. Later, the Giants were looking for a general manager, and Shula helped get him the job.

Schnellenberger, meanwhile, coached for Shula as an assistant before moving on to the University of Miami, where he brought that football program back to the top. This made him a hot property in the coaching business.

I wasn't quite sure what to do with Robert's information. Over the years, Al Davis of the Oakland Raiders has been a good friend to me, and sometimes, a confidant. I respect Al Davis as much as anyone in the game. I called him up and talked with him about what I had heard. He said, "Let me handle it." He told me to just keep coaching hard and to do the best I could, and things would work out.

Al called Jimmy "The Greek" Snyder. Jimmy was working with Brent Musburger, Irv Cross, and Phyllis George on the big pregame show on television with CBS. In those days, a lot of news about the league came on this show from Jimmy. Well, for the next three or four weeks after I spoke with Al, Jimmy went on the air saying that the Giants were trying to get rid of me. I was a talented young coach, he said. What a shame it was. I can only guess that this backed them away from Schnellenberger because the Giants came out and denied the story. In the end they didn't fire me, which as far as football goes, was just about the luckiest thing that ever happened to me.

We had an off week with a bye when Robert died. We still had some practice sessions scheduled, but I took the day off to attend his funeral. I hired a private jet and flew to Orlando for the service. It was heart wrenching. I met with Dixie Fraley and Tracey Stewart, and that was rough. They were so strong, and I was crying. When you have been through so much with a man that was supportive in so many important times in your life, it is really hard to keep it together.

Dan Reeves came. Joe Gibbs. Frank Thomas. Cortez Kennedy showed me something, taking the day off from practice in Seattle to fly all the way across the country and then back again.

When I returned to New York, practice was over, and it was hard getting back to football. The loss in Oakland the Sunday before was one of the toughest I ever had to take in my career. We played very well for forty-five minutes and then gave it up. We were ahead, 20–3, at one point in the second half, and the way our defense had been playing for the past month, I felt good about our chances. Then we fell apart. First, Tim Brown beat Aaron Glenn, our best cover guy, easily for a touchdown.

Then, and this is in my opinion the real key play of the game, Oakland had the ball with about five minutes left to play. We were ahead, 20–10. They had a third and eighteen yards to go. If we stopped them on this play, they would have to punt the ball, and by the time they got the ball back, they wouldn't have sufficient time to score enough points to beat us.

But what happened next is typical of what has killed us this season. They dropped back to pass. We bring pretty good pressure. The quarterback didn't have any extra time. He had to get rid of the ball. Our linebacker James Farrior suddenly got a brain cramp. His responsibility in the defense we have on this play is to cover the curl area. For some reason, he decided not to do that. He started drifting toward the sideline where some Raider is running a five-yard out pattern. Common sense tells you they are not going to throw a five-yard pass when they need eighteen. They completed the pass in the curl area where Farrior was supposed to be, got a first down, and kept the drive alive. This led to another score.

Now we are just up by three, 20–17. But we put together a pretty good drive and held the ball for three or so minutes, and kicked a field goal to get ahead by six, 23–17.

I like my chances, up by six, with a minute and forty seconds to go. On the kickoff, they get penalized back to their own ten-yard line, so now they have to drive ninety yards. A field goal doesn't do them any good. They have to score a touchdown.

Their drive was a nightmare for us. Ten times—and we counted them from the film of the game—we had a chance to make a play that would have stopped the drive and won the game for us. Ten times we couldn't make a single play. Ten times. Some of the things we did were inexcusable. We let Brown catch a twenty-five-yard pass when we had him double covered. Double covered.

Their winning touchdown was a killer. Their quarterback went back to pass. We had two guys on him right away. They should have had the sack. Both guys missed him. Then he threw a pass that went right through the hands of one of our defensive backs to the receiver for the winning touchdown.

This year there are more close games in this league than ever before. So many of them come down to the fourth quarter. We could have, and should have, won the last four games. But we gave all of them up at the end.

What I'm finding out is that our defense is not as good as I thought it was or thought it was going to be. When the game is on the line, our defense can't make the play for us to win it. It's doing the things a losing team does. When you give up a third and eighteen, give up touchdowns to double coverage, miss chances to sack the quarterback, let the quarterback end up being the leading rusher on the other team because you can't contain him, then you are going to lose close games. I think some of the guys we have on defense are losing their confidence and are afraid to try to make a big play.

That's the difference this year between us and a team like Miami. The Dolphins went into Oakland last Sunday, a week after us. They had a six-point lead like we did when Oakland got the ball back at midfield with a couple of minutes to play. Miami had a tougher deal. Oakland had to go ninety yards on us, and just fifty on them. But their defense made the play. They sacked the quarterback twice in a row, and the game was over. They went back to Miami a winner.

We've got Arizona coming to town this week, and we should beat them. New England worked them over in Arizona last Sunday, 27–3. Jake Plummer is out, and they don't have much offense without him, and they have the youngest offensive line in the league.

I told the team I don't care if our record is 1 and 6, we can still beat any team we have left on our schedule. I was being honest. Arizona. New England. Buffalo. Miami. None of them scare me. In fact, there isn't a team in this league this year that scares me.

The positive thing about our team is they are still competing hard. I have no bitch about their effort. Our special teams have been great. I think we have the best team in the league on kick-offs, both ways. Our punting game with Tupa has been outstanding. We've had only forty-two penalties as a team, which is the same as we had a year ago this time.

The difference between last year, when we were very good, and this year, when we are not very good, is on offense. Last year we were scoring twenty-five points a game. This year it's sixteen. This year we are giving up twenty points a game, last year it was seventeen. Third down has been killing us. We have been converting something like 30 percent of the time, which is awful. Our opponents have been converting third down around 47 percent of the time, which is awful on our part.

So we focused on our weaknesses during this bye week. We went in pads three days. Every day we have done the same thing. Third-down offense. Third-down defense. Short-yardage offense. Short-yardage defense. All three days. In pads. Players don't like to put on pads in the bye week. They think it's kind of like a vacation. But when you are 1 and 6 there is no vacation. We're not going to use this time to rest. We are going to use it to get better.

When I met with the team I gave them some new short-term goals. First for the Cardinals game, and then for the rest of the year. I told them offensively, we have to add seven more points and take it up from sixteen to twenty-three. We need to get third down up to 40 percent from 30. I want fifty more yards per game passing. That means either two more good completions a game, or four more mediocre completions per game. Wayne Chrebet is coming back from his injury, so he alone should improve our passing game about 35 or 40 percent. He opens up the field for us and provides more versatility. Arizona's defense won't be able to focus their attention on Keyshawn as much as other teams have. Finally, I want one fewer penalty per game on offense. I don't think that is asking for a lot.

Defensively, I want to hold the opposition to three points less per game. I want to take 10 percent off third down, from 47 to 37. I want to keep the other team under 100 yards rushing. We've been giving up about 120 rushing yards per game.

We're starting to catch a little flak in the press about problems on the team. Unnamed players giving out quotes about
this and that. I don't see or hear of any problems on this team.
There have been no discipline problems during the season. The
players are showing up on time. There is no division within the
team, and the players still seem happy with one another.
There's no denying all of us are frustrated.

I've got a situation on my hands right now that could be a
problem. We've got the league looking to suspend Jason
Ferguson for steroids, and I know he is not a steroid user. How
do I know? He is 315 pounds and doesn't have a muscle in his
body. What he is . . . is not smart. But there are a lot of guys on
this team, and in this league, who are not smart when it comes
to food supplements. They are ignorant when it comes to taking
this stuff. They go into stores looking for products to help them
either gain more muscle or lose weight. That was the case with
Jason. He wanted to lose weight because I was getting on his
case for being too heavy. So he starts to take stuff to help him
out, then winds up getting a letter from the league telling him he
is going to be suspended.

He has appealed. Now he has to send the product along so the
league can test it to see if it has any properties that would test
like steroids. The product was unregulated. We're sitting here
hoping that the test will back him up. There's nothing about
steroids or steroidlike properties on the label. The league has to
do a better job about educating these kids about what they can
and can't take, and about which items that can be bought over
the counter will get them in trouble with NFL testing.

If this kid is suspended for steroids it's a joke.

Steve Gutman talked to me this week about some of the meetings he has had with Goldman Sachs about the people wanting
to buy the team. I heard there are five or six potential buyers,
and a couple more playing poker, two guys who might just get
in at the end but don't want their names mentioned until they

make up their minds. I told Steve that when they have the bidders down to the ones who might be the real deal, if he or Goldman Sachs wants me to, I will talk to them about the team and give them honest answers to anything they want to know. If they want to talk to me about my future as well, that's fine, too. I will listen to what they have to say, but as far as my immediate future is concerned, I haven't made any decisions.

Rick Mirer

NOVEMBER 11, 1999

We finally won a game. We beat Arizona, 12–7, a little reward for the players and coaches who have been working hard.

It wasn't the kind of win I was looking for though. I thought with the bye week, getting some players healthy, and playing Arizona, which has come upon hard times, we might have a breakout game on offense. It didn't happen. We had our chances, but Mirer just can't seem to pull the trigger.

We have the Patriots in New England next Monday night, so I'm going back to Ray Lucas at quarterback, hoping he can give us a lift.

Rick hasn't been helping the other team with turnovers. He's been pretty good that way. But he hasn't been helping us the way he should with the opportunities he had. With this passing game we're just not going to win many games. We damn near lost this one. They had us down late in the game and Rick threw a bomb to Keyshawn to win the game for us. But we should have never been in that situation. We should have had the game put away by then.

The first question at the press conference after the game was, "Do you think the game plan was conservative?" When I said no they asked why. I told them: "We called nineteen passes in the first half but the quarterback only threw ten of them. He was sacked twice and pulled the ball down seven more times." That's one of the major reasons I'm sitting Rick down and going with

Lucas. Rick is to the point where he doesn't want to take a chance. He's lost his confidence. When you are not making plays in the passing game you cannot take control of the game. No matter how error free you are playing, the other team eventually will come back and take control and you will lose. We're just playing ebb-and-flow football. You can only win those kind of games when the other team is doing the same thing, and that's what happened with Arizona. They couldn't take control either.

I'm not certain that this quarterback change is going to generate more points. I'm really not. And it might hurt us because Ray is more aggressive than Rick and will probably be more prone to turning the ball over than Rick has been. By the same token, I know Ray's mental framework. He's more aggressive. He will try to press the defense more than Rick has been doing. Now, can he do it well? Can he get us more points? I don't know. Wish I did. Will he make a difference in how we will play? I'm not sure. But I have to find out.

Rick has been in there a long time now, and the pattern has stayed the same. We've been in every game. We've had a chance to win every game. But we haven't won enough of them. I'm not interested in competing and still losing. That doesn't do anything for me. I would rather take a higher risk and win.

Rick has been hard to figure. As a coaching staff, we've been running some of this offensive stuff for ten years or more. Before the ball is snapped on a play we have an idea what the coverages are going to look like. We have an idea of where the ball should go and how it should get there. Then when we sit there and see that it doesn't happen, we're baffled.

Let me give you an example.

We had a situation early in the game against Arizona where we called a pass play. The pattern would have Wayne Chrebet running a ten-yard out cut. In our pregame preparation as a coaching staff, we felt this play would be effective because of the way Arizona plays defense in certain situations.

Before the ball was snapped, I could see from the sideline, and my staff could see from the press box, that we had the defense we hoped for. Chrebet should be open. It was first down. I think we were on about our own thirty-five. Arizona ran a linebacker blitz. We had a little trouble with our blocking protection, but it wasn't a major factor. The play was still there. But Rick pulled the ball down and ran. When he came to the sideline I asked him what happened.

"Well," he said, "I got some pressure from the strong side and I didn't get time to focus."

I said to him, "Okay. That's good. But we're going to run this again. This is a good play for us today."

Well, the next period, maybe seven or eight minutes later, we were in the red zone, inside their twenty, looking to go in for a score. We thought the play will work again. Same situation. Same coverage. We saw it all presnap. What happens? Rick did the very same thing. He pulled the ball down and didn't throw it.

Again I asked him what happened.

"I just didn't think I could get the ball to him," he answered.

I asked, "Well, why didn't you think you couldn't get the ball to him?"

"I just didn't think I could get the ball to him."

The whole design of this play has been to get the ball to that receiver. That's why we've been practicing this play in preparation for this game. That's why he's been running the play hundreds of times in practice during the season. We've seen Rick execute this play in practice with no problems. But under the pressure of an actual game, something is happening to him. He can't make it happen. I'm at a loss to explain why.

Vinny Testaverde, who sits with the coaches in the press box during games, listens to everything that's going on. He can hear all of the calls. I ask him from time to time, "Am I crazy here?" He thought there were seven or eight times in the game where we got exactly what we were looking for, and the ball didn't go there. How do you explain it?

When you look at Rick's record, he has had a pass efficiency rating in the league in the low sixties. He's thrown about twice as many interceptions as touchdowns in the course of his career.

And basically that is what he has done here. I thought he could be different with us, but he hasn't changed. He's a good kid. He's smart. He's astute. But it's just not happening for him.

And we've done everything we could, in our minds, to make it easier for Rick. To protect him a little bit, we've used a philosophy based on not getting him into third down and long situations. If we pass on first down and it goes incomplete, we run on second down, even though the chances of running for a first down are not that great. But we know we should gain something. Even a few yards, to minimize the third-down distance. In this Cardinals game, using this philosophy, we wound up with eight third and ones. You could go three weeks and not have eight third and ones. In the average game, you have two or three. It happened because of the philosophy we were using, trying to minimize third-and-long for Rick. We converted only four of those, which is very poor, and one of the reasons we've been getting beat. I've been saying all along we're lousy in short-yardage situations.

The other night Dan Henning and I were talking in my office late after practice. It was about Mirer. Dan's one of my closest friends. He doesn't have to be bashful around me. I asked him what he thought the problem was, and he told me, "It's the general manager."

Well, I'm the general manager, and he knows that. Then he asked me, "If you didn't make the trade for Rick, and if you weren't the reason Rick was with us now, would you still play him?"

Point taken. But I said I would because I'm not convinced yet that he can't do it.

But now I am convinced. There's just something missing with Rick and I can't find it. I've got to go with Lucas.

In this Arizona game the elements were a big problem. It was very windy in Giants Stadium. I went out on the field about 8:30 and it was already starting to gust. I've coached enough games in this stadium to know that by kickoff at 1:00, the flags are going to be straight out. We anticipated the wind. We spent a lot of time the night before in our meeting with the players going over wind management.

You go over all of the points you want to make. Going into the wind, milk the clock. Take as much time off the clock as you can. Then be more aggressive with the wind. Again I hit home the point that when they are punting with the wind, don't let the ball hit the ground and take a big roll. Against the wind, same thing, don't let a bouncing ball hit one of our players and cause a turnover. We were also going to try to block a couple of punts. Sometimes, snappers who are not used to these conditions don't know how to deal with it and can have problems. The snap from center with the wind will sail. Into the wind, it will react like a knuckleball and wobble. Both of these situations might provide us the opportunity of an extra second or two to get a block.

We were losing, 7–3, at halftime, and even though we didn't score in the third period, to me it was the critical time of the game. Arizona had the wind and a chance to open some distance that we probably could not have overcome, considering the way we played. But we held the ball for nine minutes, didn't let them score any more points, and used the wind and better field position to beat them at the end.

Our defense played a lot better in this game. Arizona was just 17 percent on offensive conversions on third down. This was an area we focused on trying to improve in this game. Offensively, we ran the ball well. We had over 180 yards rushing in the game, and with that kind of rushing yardage you should be scoring thirty points, but we couldn't play a complementary game with our pass offense. We missed one pass play wide open for a touchdown. We missed another that had a chance to be a touchdown. When we scored and went ahead, 12–7, we went for a two-point play. It was a play we had a lot of repetitions with in practice. But Rick did not do a good job of executing it, and it failed.

Dave Brown, the former Giant, played quarterback for the injured Jake Plummer, and like Mirer he struggled in the wind.

It was tough to throw, but I've seen tougher in this stadium, which can be one of the most difficult stadiums in the league to throw in successfully on a windy day.

In 1986, when I was coaching the Giants in the NFC championship game against Washington, the wind was gusting forty-five miles an hour. That was the worst I've seen. We beat them, and a lot of it had to do with the ability of our quarterback, Phil Simms, to throw the ball effectively in the wind. If your quarterback can throw a nice tight spiral, with a lot of rotations, without wobbling, then you have a chance. Phil could do that. Vinny can do that. Phil and Vinny would both drop down a little bit in their throwing motion. Not so much over the top like they regularly do. More three-quarters, with more spin. This produces a tighter spiral and better accuracy in windy conditions. This kind of ability makes a quarterback weatherproof.

But there are some quarterbacks who simply can't change their motion and still be accurate. With others their hands are too small, or their natural throwing motion is such that the ball is going to wobble no matter what. Throwing the ball well in the wind is not something that just happens. Quarterbacks have to find out through practice what their particular passes are going to do in the wind, both with and against. If you have a quarterback who plays most of the time indoors in a domed stadium, or a passer who is not used to throwing in the wind, he has a tough time. In our championship game in Denver last year, it was very windy, yet Vinny hit something like fourteen of his first fifteen passes while John Elway was struggling.

We had something of a situation before the Arizona game. With the bye on our schedule, we had two weeks off between games and practiced quite a bit. But on Friday, just two days before the game, Eric Green says to our trainer, not me, that his knee was bothering him and he didn't think he could play. We'd been together two weeks and he hadn't said anything. He took almost all of the snaps in practice. Then forty-eight hours before kickoff, we get the word. If he had told me sooner, I would've gotten Baxter ready to play. Let's just say I wasn't happy.

Spence, one of my other tight ends, had a dislocated finger and wasn't going to be able to play. That meant Baxter was our only healthy tight end. I had already put Spence's name into the league as inactive. We had to call the league office and change that before it was too late. We also had to get a kid named Jermaine Wiggins off our practice squad and ready to play if Green could not. I waited until 7:00 Friday night, the only night I have to myself all week, for Green to come back from seeing the doctor. When he finally showed up I asked him what the deal was. I said, "Can you at least play backup for me behind Baxter?"

"I'm not sure I can," he said.

"Tell me whether you can or you can't," I told him. "That's what I want to know. It doesn't make any difference, but I have to know what you are going to do, because if you can't, I have to make other arrangements."

After I mentioned that Spence was injured, he said he hadn't realized that, and that he could play backup. So I dressed him. He was in about five or six plays.

Eric doesn't know where he is in his career. He can't play anymore, and he doesn't want to accept that. I want him to do some things, but he just can't keep up. He thinks it's personal, but he's been a disappointment to me and the team.

Now I have to get the team ready to play in New England on Monday night, and listen to more of this Tuna Bowl crap for another week. I really don't want to deal with it, but I know the press will bring it up. Personally, I don't give a shit emotionally that we are playing New England. That stuff is all over. Now they are just another team that I want to try to beat.

This will be my third game back in New England since I left. The first one was wild. There was a lot of excitement, with people holding up signs and yelling stuff. Last year wasn't as bad.

The fans will razz me a little bit, but I just block it out. It's nothing like I used to get when I would go into Washington or Philly with the Giants. Now, those people were really tough.

When I went to New England, the team was down, with the worst record in the league and plenty of empty seats. By the time I left we had rejuvenated the team, with sold-out games and a trip to the Super Bowl. It's been very competitive for a good period of time now, and I think it will continue to be. And as long as you stay competitive, you always have a chance to win.

I still know a lot of New England's core guys, and I like to visit with them on the field before the game. I have strong personal feelings for them, and it's good to see many of them still playing and being successful. New England has as good a shot as any team right now to win this whole thing. Bledsoe is playing as well as anyone in the league. Offensively, they are very strong, and they live by the pass. They put up impressive numbers with their wide receivers. I think their wide receivers as a group have caught something like 103 passes, with better than a seventeen-yard average per catch, which is exceptional.

Bledsoe plays better each time I see him. His confidence continues to grow. He's more poised, making better decisions, and will take a hit to wait for the long ball to come open. He's done a lot of that. I think he's been knocked down more than any other quarterback in the league at the midpoint of the season.

Defensively, they've got five or six guys who are very talented. Law and Milloy in the secondary. Linebackers McGinest and Slade are having their best seasons in a couple of years. Their kicking game is very good.

Miami's in first place now, but that isn't going to last unless they can get Marino back. They're playing in Buffalo this week, and I think they will get beat there. If Miami wins, then I will change my mind. But I don't think that is going to happen. Those four teams—Miami, Buffalo, New England, and the Colts—will be in this thing to the finish.

No one gives us a chance in New England in this game, but we've got a shot. What I try to do as a coach is bring high energy to practice and the meetings, letting the team know that regardless of what our record is, we're playing to win. We practice that way. And we will play that way.

We have to play a complementary game. We can't get stuck on the field all night on defense. We have to run some time off the clock when we have the ball. I feel good about our special teams. I think we can gain the edge on them in field position in our kicking game. But if we don't stop Bledsoe from completing thirty-yard passes, we'll get our butts kicked. We can't get into a shoot-out. We have to make them work for everything they get.

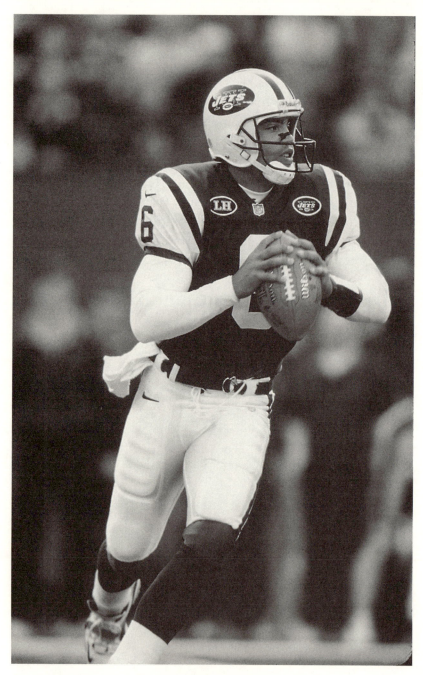

Ray Lucas always provides a spark for the team.

NOVEMBER 18, 1999

We had a hell of a win in New England, even though it was all stacked against us. As a coach, there are three things you don't want to see when you receive the schedule from the league office each April. You don't want to play: (1) on the road, (2) at night in a hostile environment, (3) against a tough division opponent. This is the third year in a row we've had to play a night game in Foxborough. Maybe someone should talk to our television committee about that and see if it isn't time we have a little change.

On top of all this they were playing very well going into the game, and we were not. And they were coming off a bye week, well rested. So let's swap positions and take the Patriots' side. They've had two weeks off, they're playing well, they've got the home game at night with a fired-up crowd going behind them. Not bad.

Coaches hate to play at night on the road. The entire schedule is out of whack compared to what you are doing most of the weeks during the season. When you get to game day, you want to get it over with. I'd play them all at 10:00 in the morning if I had my way. Everyone hates to hang around all day waiting. It kills you. At least if you are at home for a night game you can keep busy and find things to do to take your mind off the game for a while. On the road, you are stuck in the hotel just watching the clock, anxious as hell to get out of there and get to the stadium.

When we get to the stadium, I find another deal I'm not too happy with: the officiating crew they've sent to do this game. I specifically asked the league office during preseason not to give me this crew for any game during the regular season. I've been coaching in this league for a long time, and it's the first and only time I have ever done that. It's Bernie Kukar's crew, and I have nothing against him. I think he's a good official who has worked Super Bowls.

But this year they put a couple of young guys with him, new to the league, and it has hurt that crew. They don't yet work well together, which can lead to problems. In our exhibition game one of those guys called seven penalties. Three of them were wrong. After that game I called Jerry Seeman, the head of officials, in the league office and said to him: "I don't know if it's me . . . or them. It could be me. But it's just better that we don't have this crew again."

Now I have a rule: I never bitch about officiating. I just never do. It doesn't do any good. During a game I don't want to be fighting two opponents. I just want to fight the guys on the other side of the field, not the guys in the striped shirts, because that becomes very distracting. On the sideline against New England, I just didn't have any confidence in this crew. We had a lot of big calls that all seemed to go against us.

Early in the game, when there was no score, we were driving for a touchdown when there was an offensive interference called against Keyshawn Johnson. They show the replay up on the big screen at the end of the stadium, and it sure looked like it should have been the other way. Defensive interference against Ty Law. Luckily, we overcame the penalty and scored a touchdown anyway.

At the kickoff, the official who made the call had to come past our bench. I said to him: "The replay looked like defensive interference."

"Well, he ran into the defensive guy and pushed off," he answered, "and the defensive guy was trying to recover."

"I don't think you are going to like the call when you see it on film," I said.

Having seen the call on film again, I could see why he made the call. It was close. But in my opinion it was the wrong call.

The play I really objected to was a touchdown catch by Quinn Early in the end zone. They called it a touchdown and then overruled it on the replay, saying he didn't have control of the ball. We had two important plays overturned by replay that night. They were right on one of them, a catch that Wayne Chrebet made in front of our bench where the ball hit the ground first. They were wrong with Quinn Early. His hands and arms were under the ball all the way.

I wasn't happy with the way they managed the game. Once New England called back-to-back time-outs. You can't do that. But they didn't notice and didn't penalize New England. Things like that started to bother me. I'm trying to coach my team and now I have to worry about whether or not the referees are on top of things.

When we played Arizona the week before, Ron Blum's crew came out with Al Jury, and I was totally relaxed. I have seen these guys call games for years. I know they're pros. We're going to get a well-managed game. If anything happens in the game, I can ask Ron Blum over and get an explanation. I'll get one and a good one.

Against New England, the same young guy that called seven penalties on us in preseason called three more in this one. He's very active. I really don't want to see that guy, or this crew, for a few more years.

I was satisfied with the win, because of all the things we overcame while playing with a third-string quarterback. Ray Lucas did a fine job at quarterback. Curtis Martin had another big game, and we were able to run the ball very well to give Lucas some help. Ray gave us the spark I was looking for from that position. He was aggressive and not afraid to try to make a big play.

It's kind of fitting that this is where Ray got his first NFL victory as a starting quarterback, because it all started right there in Foxborough Stadium. I was coaching the Patriots, and one year, a day or two after the college draft, I got a call from Doug Graber, the head coach at Rutgers.

He said he had a kid who he thought could play in the NFL, a quarterback named Lucas. The kid hadn't been drafted, and no one was after him to sign him as a free agent. He was a good athlete and a good guy. I'd like him a lot, he said. He had Ray right there in his office.

I told him to put Ray on the phone. We talked a bit, and I told him to come up the next day when we were bringing in some other free agents. He said he'd be there the same day. I told him there was no need, but he insisted. Rutgers is about a six-hour drive to Foxborough. Five hours later the kid is standing in front of my desk. I notice he was dressed up, with a coat, shirt, and tie. I thought to myself, "This kid must have gone home to get dressed, and still made that kind of time getting up here."

He sat down across from my desk. "I'm a quarterback," he said. "The Edmonton Eskimos have offered me thirty thousand dollars a year to go up there and play quarterback."

"Go take it," I said. "Good luck. Go the hell to Canada, where no one will ever see you again. But if you stay here, make this team, you'll make a lot more than thirty thousand dollars. I don't know what you can play, but I'm willing to give you a chance. You can trust me on that."

He got up from his chair and paced in front of my desk for about fifteen seconds before saying, "Okay, I'm gonna trust you."

That was the beginning. We tried him at wide receiver. He covered punts. He ran down on kickoffs. In preseason I started to like the kid. There was something about him, his character. He was on our practice squad all year, but then I activated him to play special teams in the AFC championship game when we beat Jacksonville, and for the Super Bowl, when we got beat by Green Bay.

The next year, New England cut him early in camp, and I picked him up for the Jets. I knew he could help our club on special teams, and that he had an outside shot to be a quarterback. After the season was over, he came into my office and said he still had this dream of being a quarterback in the NFL.

"Trying to play quarterback full-time might run you out of this league," I said.

"I know that, but I want to try."

I said okay. That's why I really like this kid. He will take the challenge. He doesn't look for the easy way out. He's not an excuse maker. He's raw. He's green. He grew up near where I grew up, so we understand each other. We speak the same language. He gets it quick. You don't have to mince words or be sensitive with him. He doesn't understand nice, and he doesn't buy soft talk. He's a realist who just wants to know what a coach expects from him.

He's also a consummate team player. He speaks up and won't take any bullshit from anyone. No matter who it is, whether it's Vinny, or some of our top defensive guys, he makes them all come clean.

When I first got a chance to spend some time around this kid, I thought he could be special as a person. I thought he could have an impact somewhere, doing something, after football.

Last off-season I called another Jersey guy, Herb Tate. Herb was in George Bush's cabinet before he came back to Jersey to be commissioner of public safety. Herb is from Newark. Ray is from Harrison, which is considered a part of Newark. I told Herb: "I got a guy I think can make a difference. Let's get him going in the right direction."

"This kid must be special because you have never called me before on anyone." So Herb took him on, and Ray works for him in the off-season and has become his protégé. Ray wants to get into some kind of law enforcement work.

When I first told Ray what I had in mind, he challenged me. "So, you don't think I can play."

He took it the wrong way. "No, I'm not saying that," I said. "You can't play pro football all your life. I'm trying to get your ass in gear in case it doesn't work out."

Monday night, I didn't worry too much about him trying to win. This kid will always try to win, no matter what he does.

Early in the game, Chris Slade tried to rough him up a little. Shake him up. Ray went back at Chris, and both of them got into it a little bit. They are friends, but Chris wanted to see if he could shake up a young quarterback in a big Monday night game. I don't blame Chris for trying.

Before the game, Jumbo Elliott had a bad back, so we had to put a rookie, a seventh-round draft choice named Ryan Young, in there. This kid is going to be something someday. He's six foot six, 320 pounds, down from 344. He's extremely intelligent. Bright. He takes coaching well. He gets it. He played the whole game and didn't give up a sack. He also blocked very well on the run.

Speaking of the offensive line, we had another tough injury in the game. We lost Jason Fabini, our best lineman, for the season with a knee injury. This is the fourth guy we lost this year without being hit. Chrebet in preseason. Vinny. Cascadden, and now Fabini. He was blocking Willie McGinest on a pass rush, and when the play was over he just fell over backward. His knee gave out on him. So we had to put Elliott back in there, and hope his bad back held up the rest of the game.

We met most of our goals for the game. We played a real physical game. We kept their offense off the field by controlling the clock and the ball. Our defense was excellent. We did a great job of getting them off the field on third down. There were twelve first-down situations in the game, and they converted only two. And we stopped them in a critical fourth and one at the goal line.

After we went up, 7–0, they had a big punt return by Kevin Faulk inside our ten-yard line. Chris Hayes, who had been one of our best special teams players, missed a head-on tackle on Faulk at their twenty. Just clean missed it.

When fourth down and one came, we got lucky. But it was the kind of luck based on good preparation by our defensive staff. We felt the Patriots had a tendency to run left. Bill Belichick made the call, and we were able to get a great push off the defensive line by our rookie Jason Wiltz. He knocked the guy in front of him into the backfield, cutting off Terry Allen, the running back. We stopped him and the ball was ours.

I've got a good defensive coaching staff. Our players believe strongly in our coaches, who give them a chance to succeed, which is really what they want to do.

I had to get on Ray early to wake him up a little. I yelled at him when he came to the sideline after throwing a pass over Keyshawn's head. I could see he wasn't setting his feet.

"What the hell are you doing?"

"I read it the right way," he said, explaining the technical part of it. He didn't understand what I was getting at.

"I'm not talking about what you did, but about how you did it. You look antsy out there. Settle down. When you get back in there, set your feet, and throw the ball."

Afterward he told me I was right. I didn't blame him for being a little nervous about the situation the way it was, but I had to get him to calm down. He did. He played a fine, competitive game and never backed away from any situation. I was very happy for him when it was all over and he was getting some media attention. It has been a long journey for him.

We had a 24–3 lead in the third period, which to me was the key point in the game. We had scored 21 points with the wind in the second period. They had the wind in the third. We didn't want them to break out. We put together a drive that lasted over eleven minutes with nineteen plays to take control. Then we almost gave it back in the fourth.

We made some dumb plays on defense, and they scored two touchdowns. So now it was 24–17, with more than five minutes

left to play. It should not have been this close. We had a couple
of times when we could have put this game out of reach, but
we didn't do it. A penalty took away one score, and Richie
Anderson dropped a touchdown pass right in front of our bench.
When the play was over, Tedy Bruschi, their linebacker, walked
by our bench and yelled, "Bill, you had me on that one. You had
me." He was laughing. I thought it was cute, but I wasn't happy.

Now we've got Buffalo coming in here Sunday. They've
improved a lot on offense since they beat us up there the second
week of the season. I didn't think they were very good then, but
I do now. They probably have the best balance of all the teams
fighting it out to win this division.

New England and Indianapolis depend too much on offense.
New England has a better defense than Indianapolis. Miami
needs to get Dan Marino back if they want to make a run for it,
because Buffalo exposed Damon Huard last week. In their loss,
Miami barely got a hundred yards on offense. Huard looked
good in the first couple of games he played after Dan got hurt,
but I think teams are starting to realize what he cannot do and
taking advantage of it. Huard had to play in a tough place, but he
was nine of twenty-five. When that happens, your teammates
start to look at you a little bit sideways.

The test of a quarterback, and I spoke with Ray Lucas about
this, is not going out there and playing a game or two, hitting a
few passes, and everybody thinking you can do it. The test of a
quarterback is you just lost 30–7, been beat up, and thrown four
or five interceptions. The loss is primarily your fault. And everyone around you starts to lose confidence in you. How do you
respond?

What kills a lot of quarterbacks in this league is their inability
to respond to media pressure after a bad game, or a streak of bad
games. This is when they find out about themselves. The ones
that succeed and go on have whatever it takes to put all of the
scrutiny behind them and get on with doing the job of winning.
Let's see if Huard can do that. Miami is too defense reliant at this

point, but if they get some offense, they'll be in the picture all the way.

As for my kids, they haven't thrown it in one time this year. They've battled all the way.

I got on Lucas in practice yesterday, and the other players enjoyed it. Ray's feisty and doesn't like it when anyone gets on his ass.

"Fellas, do you realize we had a media darling right here in our huddle," I'd say. "A one-game wonder. How lucky are we?"

I'm still concerned about our steroid situation with Jason Ferguson. We haven't heard anything on it yet, and in this league, no news is bad news. If we lose this guy, we'll be screwed.

Jason Ferguson is our best defensive lineman. He made a dumb mistake—taking some supplements—and we're going to pay heavily for it.

NOVEMBER 25, 1999

There are times when this league really sucks, and this is one of them. It's Thanksgiving Day, but I'm so pissed off I can't see straight. Get this. The league waits until after practice—after practice!—yesterday to tell me that Jason Ferguson starts his suspension this week. They couldn't tell me yesterday? They couldn't tell me Monday? They knew on Monday exactly what they were going to do because they were already writing the news release, but they didn't tell me about it.

So we wasted time getting Ferguson ready to play a game he's not going to play. The kid who is going to take his place hasn't practiced at all. Ferguson is gone for four weeks. I know he's not guilty. They know he's not guilty, yet they ship his ass out for four games. He even took a polygraph test and passed. I told Ferguson this is his own fault. If he got himself in better shape and didn't have to fight weight all the time, this would never have happened.

All he did was buy some stuff in a store that wasn't government regulated. He didn't know what the hell he was doing. A lot of these guys don't. You need to be a damn pharmacist to figure it all out. But I know that he did not willfully ingest steroids or take anything to enhance his performance. I know enough about this kid to know at least that much. No one can tell me any different.

But the league policy is the league policy, so they have to suspend him. They have no other recourse. And the league knows it has a bad policy about this stuff right now. It has happened to three or four kids that are not steroid guys, but they have a rule that when it's applied to the letter, you end up punishing kids who are not guilty.

Jason appealed the ruling, and they basically came back and told him: we're stuck, we have to enforce the rule. Which is okay. But that hearing was two weeks ago, and they knew what they were going to do, but they don't tell me until 3:20 Wednesday afternoon, the day before Thanksgiving, when we're playing the first-place team in our division the coming Sunday.

They put us in a competitive disadvantage by doing this, and I take exception to it. It wasn't right. The Giants had a kid put out for steroids this week, and they told them on Sunday. Detroit had a kid put out for a late hit, and they told them on Tuesday. So those two teams knew earlier in the week than we did.

This league hates me. They're still upset that I got Curtis Martin from New England. They think I pulled a fast one on them, so every time they get a chance they try to stick it to me.

I don't think I pulled anything. When we got Curtis Martin as a free agent, we did it by working out a contract we didn't think the Patriots would match. By the rules, they had the chance to match and keep him. But the league didn't like it. They hadn't seen a contract like it before. But they had to approve it, because it was all done within the rules of the Collective Bargaining Agreement. After okaying it, they grandfathered it in to prevent any more contracts like it in the future. So now I think the league has a little bit of a chip on its shoulder about us. We even wanted to restructure Keyshawn Johnson's contract a few months back, and they wouldn't go along with it.

Now we have to play Indianapolis, probably the best offensive team in the league right now, without my best defensive lineman. Also, Brian Cox, one of my best defensive players, can hardly play. He's been hurt, and trying his ass off, but he just can't play the way he is capable of. The injury is hernia-related.

A lot of hockey and soccer players get it, and Curtis Martin had his last year in New England. I think Cox played eleven plays last Sunday when we beat Buffalo, and he is usually in a game for around thirty-five plays. He's to the point where he just can't do it anymore.

And I've got a bad situation on offense at tackle. My two starting tackles, Fabini and Young, are gone. Young was playing real well this year for a rookie, but he was injured in the game and joins Fabini on the Injured Reserve. Now I've got to go find someone who can play tackle for us this week. Jumbo Elliott will be one, but he's still bothered by a bad back, and we can't count on how long he can last.

I now have nine guys out of the lineup who have no chance to play. Testaverde, my quarterback. Leon Johnson, third-down back, kick returner. Both offensive tackles, Fabini and Young. Eric Green at tight end. Otis Smith at corner. Ferguson in the defensive line. Chas Cascadden, linebacker. And Cox, who is one of the best defensive players in the league when he is healthy, but who is now hardly able to go.

But I'm really proud of my team. The players were tough and resilient against the Bills last week. When we played in Buffalo at the start of the year, they ran the ball all over us. I said if we had had Ferguson that night—he was out with a bad knee—that wouldn't have happened. He played this game and we shut their running game down. They got nothing.

We didn't make any mistakes. We didn't turn the ball over. They turned it over three times. We reversed what happened in Buffalo. We ran the ball only eighteen times in Buffalo, but thirty-four here. They ran it only seventeen times. We put a lot of pressure on Flutie and forced him into some mistakes. Our special teams made two big plays, downing the ball on punts deep in their territory. We got seven points out of one, and three points out of another. We had all the elements to win. Field position. Clock control. No turnovers. I've been telling my team, as banged up as we have been, that if we win the battle in these three areas, we will win the game.

We got up, 17–0, and that played into our hands. They had to get away from the running game, which is what they do best, spread out the field, and depend on Flutie's passing. That's not the way they prefer to play. And when they spread out, that opened up some lanes for our defense to pressure him. That gave us a better chance to blitz. We knew we could rush more guys at him than they could block. The only problem with Flutie when you blitz him is that you have to make sure he doesn't get out of the pocket and start to run. Then he's real dangerous. So your blitz has to occupy all possible escape lanes for him, and the defense must stay disciplined. He only got out once all day, and ran for twenty yards. Other than that, he didn't hurt us.

We handle Flutie well. In the four games he has played against us in the last two years, they've never scored more than seventeen points, and in the other three it was seven, ten, and twelve points. When you hold a team under seventeen you should win.

I got a memo on my desk that came in from the league office about this taunting stuff, which Keyshawn Johnson probably triggered. When we beat the Patriots in New England on Monday night, they showed him on television making that throat-slashing gesture after he scored a touchdown. Then some other guys picked up on it and started to do it. Now it's become a big deal.

Here's an excerpt from the memo:

Prior to this season, NFL players were notified of the impor-tance that this office places on the maintenance of high standards of professionalism and sportsmanship, and that disciplinary action could result from unsportsmanlike conduct by players during an NFL game.

The heart of the memo says that gestures considered abusive or insulting will not be tolerated, and the players will be fined. I'm all for that. There's too much of this crap going on.

Years ago I was coaching the Giants when the Fun Bunch in

Washington started to popularize celebrating in the end zone after a score. Those kids had fun with it, and I don't object to fun. But too many players in this league have taken it beyond that. I told Keyshawn I didn't like it, and he says he won't do it anymore.

I told my guys not to do any of this stuff long before this happened. But these kids nowadays do what they see. If someone else gets away with it, then they are going to try it. Players started to take their helmets off all the time after they made a play to make sure everyone knew who did it. The league outlawed that and made it a penalty, so it's not done anymore. In the last couple of years, Terrell Davis started saluting after a touchdown, so everyone else started saluting. Some of it was done against Denver to mock their players. So though they take away the throat-slashing move, it will be something else next.

I don't like anything that happens on the field like that to get the crowd stirred up. I feel strongly about this. Violence, and doing things to trigger violence, is getting out of control in this league and making me concerned. People are profane. They are malicious. They are insulting. Every year it gets worse. It has gone way beyond where it was when I first began coaching. We better put a stop to it or we might have a few riots on our hands like they do in Europe in soccer.

I didn't watch it myself, but they had a bad scene in Denver Monday night with the Raiders. The Bronco fans started throwing snow and ice at the Oakland players, pelting them with it, and when the game was over a couple of Oakland players went after the fans. Now that could have really gotten out of control. It's not just in the NFL. I watch some of these college games on television and it's much more physical and verbal in the stands than it ever was when I was coaching college ball.

We've got a tough job on our hands this Sunday—the Colts in Indianapolis. They're tied for first place right now at 8 and 2. We should have beat them here earlier in the year. That's the game we were going in for the win late in the game, and Ray Lucas threw an interception, and they took it the other way to beat us on a field goal.

Here's what I think we have to do to beat them. Our general game plan will be to hold the ball for thirty-four minutes, win the turnover battle, and prevent big plays for their wide receivers. I need one big play on special teams. The Colts like to jump on everyone early with their offense and keep firing away. I wish we had more offense to fire back with. We are going to need to score more than seventeen points to win this one. These guys can move the ball.

Usually, the crowd in Indianapolis is not a problem. They haven't had a lot to cheer about the last couple of years. But considering the way their club is playing and that the game will be played in a domed stadium, we're going to work a lot on crowd noise in practice this week.

Jim Mora's done a hell of a job coaching this club. I always have liked Jim. I thought he did a real good job in New Orleans. I think he has handled Peyton Manning the best possible way. They protect this kid well with their blocking schemes. They don't leave him exposed. Too many promising young quarterbacks, including his father, Archie, have been beat up too young in this league by coaches who didn't protect them the way they should have. Peyton is a very good quarterback, and he is going to be even better.

Manning has a couple of very good players with him. Marvin Harrison, their top wide receiver, is the most productive in the AFC. They work very well together. I didn't think they could replace Marshall Faulk when they traded him to St. Louis just before the draft, but they have come close to it with their rookie running back, Edgerrin James. I credit not only him, but also their offensive coordinator, Tom Moore. He's really done a good job of putting all these pieces together and integrating James into the system.

The big deal before the draft was which back was better, Ricky

Williams or James. I liked James better. He is the more complete player. He can run and block, and catches the ball better. Williams just ran the ball, and I thought he would have a weight problem.

This is going to be an emotional day for a lot of reasons. John Hess is going to speak to the team, following the tradition of his father. It will be very nostalgic. With the sale of the team coming soon, this will be the last time a Hess will ever do this. It's the end of an era.

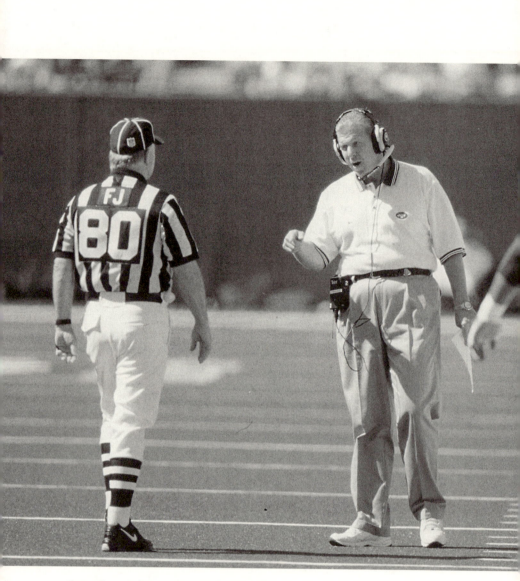

Sometimes I don't agree with officials.

DECEMBER 1, 1999

We lost another heartbreaker and I got the first penalty of my career. How's that for a daily double.

I've said since the start of the season that with so many important players beat up, we have no margin for error. We're not going to have a run at the championship that all of us envisioned before the first game, but we still have an outside chance to have a winning season, and maybe even slip into the last playoff spot.

All of that was over on Sunday. Now, as coaches, we're facing a new challenge. We know, and the players know, that it is virtually impossible to make the playoffs, so our job as a staff, and my job as the head coach, is to make sure our players go as hard as they can right to the wire.

I'm proud of these kids, though. Almost all of them have given me everything they had, and in my heart, I really feel that no matter what the circumstances are the rest of the way, they'll continue to do so because I've got a lot of good guys on this team. They want to win as much as I do, but they realize that we almost have to play a perfect game to do it.

We could have taken the Colts. They have the best overall record in the AFC and are a good team, but not a great team. We lost 13–6, but we should have scored three touchdowns in the game.

On our first possession, we had Keyshawn wide open, ten yards behind anyone else, and we overthrew the pass. On the final play of the game, Ray Lucas made a tremendous throw under pressure and Wayne Chrebet dropped the pass in the end zone. It would have tied the game and sent it into overtime. I would have liked our chances at that point. But it didn't happen. Nine times out of ten, Wayne makes the catch. He's got a great pair of hands and the ball hit him right there. Don't get me wrong, it wasn't the easiest catch to make—he had to leave his feet to go up and get it—but he still should have had it.

Another time in the game, Lucas had our tight end, Fred Baxter, wide open for a touchdown and overthrew him. Instead of being up 14–0 in the second period like we should have been, we had to kick two field goals, and had only six points. At 14–0, we have a different ball game. We could have dictated what was going to happen a little more.

Our defense played great once again. This is a high-powered offense, and we held them to thirteen points.

We had ten penalties in the game, which has not been like us lately, and I had one of them. That was the first time it ever happened to me in the NFL. The Colts had the ball and tried a pass over the middle. Victor Green made a great play on the ball and knocked the pass away. Incomplete. Then all of a sudden a flag comes from thirty yards away, from the side judge. We've got two officials right on the spot where this action occurred, the umpire and the field judge, and they called it incomplete. But here comes the side judge, throwing the flag and calling interference on Green to give them a first down. This is not even supposed to be his call.

It was a ridiculous call by a guy who shouldn't have been involved. I got upset with him and called him an asshole. I really shouldn't have done that, and I apologized to him a few minutes later. But his call really sucked. He gave me a penalty for unsportsmanlike conduct, which I deserved. When you have no margin of error, though, and you are the underdog fighting an uphill battle against a team with a better record on their home field, things like that happen. It's no excuse. I should have had better control of myself.

I've watched the film of the play a couple of times since, and it's still a ridiculous call. No way it should have been a penalty. None. Green never touched the guy. In fact, he positioned his body in a way to purposely avoid contact with the receiver and then reached his right hand around in front of him and knocked the ball away. Cleanly. But the ball went back to them. Instead of us getting it back, they kept it and went downfield to get a field goal.

Indianapolis has been averaging thirty points a game against the rest of the league, but not against us. They scored sixteen the first game and thirteen in this one. They have twenty-nine points in two games against us, when they are averaging thirty a game against everyone else. We should have won both those games with that kind of defensive performance, but we didn't.

For the first time all year, we had major problems with our offensive line, and it showed. With Fabini and Young out, we were down to one offensive tackle, Jumbo Elliott. He had a bad back and was questionable. So we had to find a guy: Siupeli Malamala. Right off the street. The kid hadn't played in two years. We grabbed him for three reasons. First, he lived right here on Long Island. Second, he was in good shape. And third, he had been with us before, so he knew what the offense was all about. He is a good kid. He's strong. He has a lot of heart, and most importantly, he was free.

Now, to illustrate how bad we are on offense this year, he played the whole game. Hadn't played in two years, but he can start and play the whole game for us at tackle. Under the conditions, he did okay. He hurt us a little, but you have to expect that. With all of the money we charge for tickets, and all the money we have coming into the league, something like this should never happen.

Ray Lucas didn't play as well as he had been playing. He was twelve for twenty-three in passing. He didn't execute well. However, I will say this for him, in the final minute of the game he made a good throw in a clutch fourth-down situation to keep us alive. And then with the game on the line, he made a great throw to Chrebet. He's managing the game better. He's playing with a little more confidence. But he's not throwing the ball well. I thought he would be more productive.

There were two or three times in the game where we had the Colts set up for the big play. We would run the ball two times in a row and get a first down. Then we'd run it two more with Curtis for another first down. Now, you know the Colts are coming up on the line of scrimmage on the next first down to stop the run. So I called a pass play. On three different occasions, we had that situation and couldn't convert. We had a penalty, or took a sack, and couldn't make the throw. It was frustrating.

We're 4 and 7, but when I look at the league stats in front of me, we don't look like a 4-and-7 team on paper. We currently are plus nine in turnovers, a stat that usually means you are playing at a playoff level. There are only seven teams in the league that have fewer penalties than us. So we are in the top 25 percent of the league, on the plus side, for penalties. What this tells me is we are not helping the other team win. We are not playing sloppy football. And these are two of the ways you try to judge the performance of the coaching staff.

We have the Giants this week, and they haven't played up to expectations either. Both of us thought we would be playoff teams, but it doesn't look that way. But there will be some special feeling to this game. There always is when these two teams meet, even if it's in the preseason. I guess it's all about bragging rights.

I'm ten years out of the Giants now, and about the only ones I know who are still there are Well Mara and Ronnie Barnes the trainer. Well called me earlier in the week and said he usually likes to come by and say hello before the game in the locker room, but thinks if he did, some people might get the wrong impression. So we talked on the phone. Well Mara is a great guy. I have the utmost respect for him. He's a true friend.

I've never said much about why I left the Giants when I did. I didn't want to leave. I loved the people and the job, but I was sick. I started to get fainting spells and arrhythmia. I went and had tests. They didn't produce any answers I was satisfied with. I took stress tests, which is generally the way you can detect any kind of heart problem, and passed with ease. No problem, they told me. But I knew there was a problem. I know my own body, and something was wrong.

I worked out a lot then, and I still work out a lot. But back then, during this period, I continued to get light-headed, feeling faint, with my heart pounding. What I didn't know, and what the doctors couldn't detect at the time, was that I had a blocked artery in my heart.

In May, I took another physical, and this time the doctor said there could be something wrong. He told me to give up smoking, which I did and I haven't smoked since then. So I got out of coaching and went to NBC. But even on television, the same things continued to happen. I'd feel light-headed, and my heart would start to pound. At times I felt it was going right through my chest.

Finally, the following December, a test showed the blockage. I went in for angioplasty surgery right away. It didn't take. I had another one in February that didn't take. In June, I had bypass surgery, and that has turned out well.

When I look back, I think that if I had continued to coach that next season with the Giants, I probably would have had a heart attack and died right there on the sideline. I firmly believe that. I was lucky. The artery that was blocked controlled 40 percent of the blood flow. After the operation, I asked the doctor, "Suppose I had had the heart attack, what were my chances?" He told me fifty-fifty at best. I don't like those odds.

That wasn't the end of my heart problems. When I went back to New England the following football season I continued to get some arrhythmia. It became very unsettling. The doctors told me these bouts were adrenaline induced. My body was producing too much of it and I had to be careful. They gave me different medication, then they gave me more medication. It started to bother me mentally. I had some bad episodes in New England. One game in Kansas City, I thought I was going down right in front of the bench. It got so bad, I had to drop to one knee. As soon as the game was over, the doctors had to work with me in the dressing room. It was hot, and I was dehydrated. Another time, I was running on the treadmill one day after practice, and the arrhythmia got real bad. They had to get me into Mass. General Hospital for another set of tests. Nothing new. I was dehydrated again.

As I'm sitting here now, I've got two huge cups of water in front of me. I'll drink them both before the morning is over. I still get the problem from time to time, but thankfully, not as bad as in the past. I'm more cautious. I pay strict attention to taking the medication, and I take it at all the right times.

We had a situation after the Colts game with Keyshawn that I didn't care for but want to talk about to give you an idea of how things can be blown out of proportion in this business. Allegedly, after the tough loss when Chrebet dropped the last pass, Keyshawn was knocking him in a story told to the New York media by some guy in Indianapolis, who supposedly heard Keyshawn say it. But when you investigate and try to find out who the guy from Indianapolis was, no one seems to know. Yet the media runs with the story, even though they don't know if anything like that ever happened. Chrebet told me he never heard anything. I don't know what his and Keyshawn's relationship is. They talk with each other on the practice field. If they have anything between them, they have never taken it to the field, and I wouldn't let them take it to the field to have it become a problem for the rest of the team.

I called Keyshawn in and told him to keep his mouth shut. We're all frustrated. He said he didn't do anything. If he did do something, I'd have fined his ass, and that would have been the end of it. That's why it is important when you are coaching to also have the power. If you tell them to shut up, and they know you have the final call, they'll shut up. But if you have an owner that won't back you up, then it's a different story. That's why I always wanted the hammer.

I'm worried about this Giants game. I don't care what their record is. They're good on defense, and this Kerry Collins kid gives them more punch at offense. We'll see what happens.

Jim Fassell's team just beat the hell out of us. It was one of the worst losses of my career.

DECEMBER 8, 1999

We played like a bunch of dogs.

I can't describe our game with the Giants any better than that. They kicked our ass every way possible, and it was so bad I've been sitting here for days now trying to figure out whether this team has gone into the tank on me or not.

After watching it in person, and looking at it again on film, I know I had at least three guys that took the day off, and a few more that are suspect.

And that really bothers me, because I take it personally. We were so bad I'm doubting myself as a coach. Maybe I should just retire.

That's only the second time in my coaching career that a team has scored forty points on us. Our defense in this game simply sucked. It couldn't play any worse than it did. This wasn't the greatest offense in the world we were playing against. We've shut down a lot better than them this year, but I can't take any credit away from the Giants. Their offense earned everything.

Usually when you get beat like that, and give up forty points, your offense has to contribute by giving the ball back on fumbles or interceptions, or giving the other team great field position for easy scores. That didn't happen. We didn't turn it over. We had only four penalties. Yet the Giants just took it every time and drove it down our throats. That's hard to swallow.

Aaron Glenn, who is supposed to be our best cornerback and a Pro Bowl–type player, had the worst day I've ever seen him have. They absolutely ate him alive in the first half. I talked to him at halftime and tried to settle him down. He had given up a touchdown and set up another with an interference penalty. I didn't yell at him, because he's a sensitive guy, and he might go into a shell and not challenge the receivers. I just told him he had to pick it up. The pass interference he had was the ninth of the season for him, an unusually high number, though not all of them were accepted. I doubt that anyone else in the league has nine. The irony here is the two best games he had all year were against Marvin Harrison of the Colts, who has been the best receiver in our conference this year, if not the best in football. Glenn had enough problems without me giving him hell.

I told our team at the half, I thought we had a shot. We were down three touchdowns, and I told the players that if we got one quick, got a touchdown in a hurry, we could get right back in this thing and win it. Only at one point in the second half, the way things turned out, did I think we had a shot to pull it out. We closed the score to 34–21. The ball was deep in their end on a third and ten. If we stopped them, and made them punt, we could have scored a quick touchdown and got it back to six. We could still win. We had enough time.

But we never got a chance to find out. We gave up another bomb for seventy or eighty yards and a touchdown. Just one play. I'm not saying we were going to win it, but if we stop them right here, we've got the chance to win it and could have made it interesting. Then we turned around and gave up another big play.

I told the team after the game in the locker room that I was ashamed. Ashamed of myself as their coach, and ashamed for them and their performance. There wasn't anyone on our side that day that could walk out of our locker room with their head held up. How could they?

Of course the players put their own spin on it. Their big line after the game was: "I didn't see any of us quitting out there."

Well, I think I did.

When we came back together as a team on Wednesday I wanted to address that subject. "One of the things you can do in this business is fool yourself," I said. "It's human nature to do so. Now, if you want to fool yourselves, go ahead. But we won't have a chance to do anything the rest of the year. Don't try to put a spin on it and the effort you made because anyone who looks at that film can see the effort wasn't there. If any of you want to dispute that, then come to me and we'll go in and watch the game together for a while."

No one did. But I didn't confront the guys either, that might have sent them into the tank on me. But I'm not forgetting it. And if I see it happen again next week with the same guys, or any game the rest of the year with the same guys, then they'll be out of here. A few of them are going to be out of here anyway. I let myself get talked into keeping one of these guys when I thought he could be a dog, and it was a mistake. He was a dog the other day.

One guy I want to give some credit to is one of our linebackers, Marvin Jones. The guy was injured a year ago, hurt his knee so bad he had surgery and was out for the season. He made seventeen tackles in this game. Seventeen tackles. You don't make seventeen tackles in a game unless you are hustling and busting your ass.

Jones had a tough surgery, and a long rehabilitation. He started around here for a whole year working in the training room to get back on the field. He's been our leading tackler. He has really produced.

On the other side, we've probably lost Brian Cox for the season, and he was our leading tackler a year ago. Brian wasn't as good for us as he was last year, but it wasn't for lack of trying. With his injury he simply can't run or move the way he would like. He's going up to Boston to see a specialist, and I'm convinced he won't be back again this season. I'm sure they'll tell him he needs surgery, and he should have that right away.

Before the game was played, I didn't have any idea we were going to come up with that kind of performance. We did not practice well on Friday, which is generally an indication they may not have been paying attention during the week. But I've had teams not practice well on the Friday before and then go out and play a great game. There were a lot of mental mistakes. I didn't pay any attention to it until I thought more about it after the game, and realized we made more mental errors in this game than we did any game all year. We had twenty-four in all, eighteen on offense and six on defense. In a normal game you have just five or six mental errors . . . total.

So this is the low point in my tenure with the Jets. This is my third season and the first time I ever questioned effort. But this is the first time since I've been here that we got to this stage of the season and we weren't fighting for something. My first year, if we won the final game in Detroit, we would have been in the playoffs. Last year we made the playoffs. A week before the Giants game we were out of it, so I wonder about what kind of impact it had on some of these guys mentally. Maybe some of them thought they really didn't have anything to play for this year. They acted like it. Especially on defense, which surprised me because we had been playing so well prior to that.

The Giants converted thirteen of nineteen first downs, and a lot of those because we just didn't tackle well. Seven or eight of those came by just a foot or so, meaning, if we did a better job of getting to the man with the ball, or bringing him down just a step sooner, they would have had to punt. This allowed them to play the game we wanted to play. We wanted to control the ball and keep it for better than thirty minutes. They had it for thirty-five. We ended up scoring twenty-eight points, but only because they played a softer defense when they had the big lead.

I was miserable when I got back to my apartment Sunday night. I didn't want to see anyone. I didn't want to talk to anyone. I was ashamed of what happened. It was the same way Monday when I went into the office. I'm thinking I've got four games to go and what if they play the rest of them like this. I won't be able to take it. I'm not going to shield this thing. I told the media my team didn't make the effort. Other coaches won't say that.

We've got Miami coming in here, and they're fighting for the playoffs. We play them twice in the next three weeks. We play Dallas in between, and then we finish with Seattle, and they'll both be battling for a playoff spot.

I bet when the season is over, we will have played the toughest schedule in the league. Right now everyone in the division, except us, has a winning record, and we have to play them twice.

My guys have been moping around since the Giants game. I'm going to back off in practice to eliminate any excuses they might have. I'll practice them in sweats, no pads. Hopefully, they'll be a little refreshed that way. No excuses about being tired, or practicing too hard this late in the season. I have to get them back mentally.

I don't think that much of Miami. I thought they were going to be better than they are, especially on defense. They are not as good on defense as I thought they would be.

Marino doesn't look that good on film. He's struggling. Some of their guys are getting older and are not playing as well as they did before. I love this guy Zach Thomas they have as linebacker. This kid really loves to play. He is all over the field making plays. He has great anticipation, and we have to find a way to deal with him.

I've also got our ownership situation on my mind. I'm told it might come down next week. From what I'm told there are three guys left who are serious contenders—Dolan, Johnson, and Ross. This Ross is a new guy, so I don't know how serious he is. I know the other two are very serious. I'm anxious to see what the next guy has to say, and how this is going to play out for me. What I do will be pretty much determined by what the next guy wants to do. But I'll say this right now: If these players play these final four games like they did against the Giants, I won't be back for sure. That will be a sign that I can't do it anymore. I don't care who you are. There is a time when you can't do it anymore, and if I think that is what is going on, then I won't hang around. I'll be gone. I've seen some guys who could really coach stay too long, and I've vowed that will never happen to me.

DECEMBER 16, 1999

We had something happen in a win over Miami last Sunday that I think will help us not only for the rest of the season but also for the future. We're struggling a little bit against Miami, but we're playing a lot better than we did in that embarrassment with the Giants, when Ray Lucas got decked by Darryl Gardener. Gardener is a big defensive tackle, not usually a good pass rusher, but he got loose and just ran over Ray. He was on the ground for quite a while, which is good.

Now, I'll explain that. If a coach in the NFL has a good relationship with his doctors, he makes sure they know enough to keep a quarterback down on the ground long enough to get the backup warmed up. This is important. Our doctors kept Ray down for a good period of time, and when they brought him to our sidelines I checked him out. He didn't look bad. I've been around this kid, so I got an idea of what he is like. He's feisty. Competitive. I've seen him get knocked around a little on special teams and still come back for more.

Well, our doctors act like they are going to take him to the dressing room. I tell them, "Get him back here." I ask the kid if he's okay, and he says he is. But lots of times in these situations, when a player gets shaken up or dinged a little bit, they're on remote control. They want to go back out and play again to make a good impression. They tell you they feel fine, but when

Playing against a great competitor like Dan Marino causes a lot of sleepless nights for coaches.

you start to question them, they don't know what the hell you are talking about.

Simms did it to me. Hostetler did it to me.

It happened one time while I was coaching the Giants against Seattle in our own stadium. It was a big game for us. We needed it for the playoffs. Chuck Knox was coaching Seattle then, and he was one of the best I ever coached against. One of the best to coach in this league, period. No matter what kind of talent he had to work with, Chuck would always keep his team in a game and give it a shot to win at the end. They were hanging on this game, and I was afraid they were going to kick a field goal at the end and beat us.

We were driving, but we needed a touchdown to put the game out of reach in the fourth quarter, when one of our tight ends, Zeke Mowatt, got knocked out. I mean he was out. They carried him off and laid him down on the bench and his eyes were closed. A couple of plays later, we moved inside the twenty-yard line. All year, when we got inside the twenty, we went to a double tight–end offense. We needed Zeke. I walked over to the bench and looked at our doctors, and yelled as loud as I could, "Wake that son of a bitch up."

Suddenly, Zeke's eyes opened. He was out cold, but he heard me yelling at him. He grabbed his helmet and ran into the game. He played four or five plays, and we scored a touchdown. After we did, Zeke walked through the end zone and into the visitors' tunnel at the end of the field. He just played two or three minutes, did a good job, but didn't know where the hell he was, and most likely, what he was doing. But he did it.

So in this game last Sunday, I said to Lucas: "Tell me what you do on this play." He told me exactly what he was supposed to do. I gave him another, even more complicated, and he did it again. I told him to get in there, but my very first call was one of the hardest plays our quarterback has to execute. He has to sprint to his right, stop, and then throw the ball all the way back across the field. He did it and threw a touchdown pass to Keyshawn that busted the game wide open.

It not only showed me that this kid is made out of what I thought he was made of when we put him in there to start, but it also earned him tremendous credibility points with his coaches and teammates. When a player does something like that, it endears him to everybody. Even the fans. If they were paying attention, they knew he had just got his ass knocked off a few minutes before and bounced back to make a great play, which was even more sensational when Keyshawn caught the ball one-handed. He had three one-handed catches in this game, which I normally don't approve of, but as long as he catches them, I'm fine with it.

Ray ended up having his best game for us. His confidence grew as the game went along. He was a little more daring with some of his throws. He ended up completing twenty-two of thirty-eight passes against a pretty good defensive team.

Now, I'm not making light of a player taking a hard hit to the head. You have to be careful. You have to be specific. You can't ask him the simplest questions. A few years ago, as the story goes, a coach wanted to find out if his quarterback could understand where he was and what he was doing after taking a hard hit. The coach asked the quarterback what his phone number was. The quarterback said it was unlisted. I don't know if it's true or not, but if it is, the coach should have asked a tougher question. Simple ones won't do. You have to make sure he has all his faculties and he isn't having any problems.

Sometimes it's easy to tell if a player is ready to take the field again. We were playing the 49ers at home in a playoff game. Jim Burt, our nose tackle, got loose and hit Joe Montana right on the chin with a pass rush. He caught Joe flush. It was only the second quarter. They took Joe to the locker room, but I wanted to know if he was going to play the second half or not. When you are in your own stadium, you have ways of finding things out, even if it's in the other team's locker room. I was told just before we went out for the second half that Montana was not going to play. I asked the person how he knew. He said that when the doctors asked Montana if he was okay, he said he was, but when they turned their backs for a second, he passed out and fell off his chair and onto the floor. He didn't come back to play, and he shouldn't have. In fact, if my memory serves me right, they had to keep him overnight in one of the New York hospitals.

Even though we won the game against Miami, and I'm certainly happy about that, it was kind of sad for me. I've always been a big Dan Marino fan. I love the way the guy competes, and he had one of the greatest arms I have ever seen. He could throw the ball to any spot on the field as well as anyone who has ever played. I've been watching him in this league since he was a rookie, and this was the first time in watching him play that he didn't have his good fastball. I know he's been having neck and shoulder problems. He's been out of the lineup for a while getting better, but it looks to me like his legs are gone. Guys like Simms and other quarterbacks tell me that the legs go first, not the arm. In order to throw a football properly, like a guy pitching in baseball, you have to have good legs. You have to drive through the ball and get your entire body into the throw. Dan didn't look like he could do that anymore. A couple passes he threw didn't have much on them. At a critical point in the game, when we were holding on to a lead in the fourth quarter, he tried to throw a sideline route. One of our guys, Omar Stoutmire, picked it off and ran it back for a touchdown. It was late in the game, and that clinched it for us. But the throw Dan made just hung up there, it didn't have the usual zip.

We didn't do a great job in this game, but I'm certainly satisfied with it. Everyone seemed like they wanted to play. We have the same kind of offensive game plan each time we play Miami because of the personnel they have. They have excellent cornerbacks, one of whom is Sam Madison, who is having a Pro Bowl kind of year, Terrell Buckley, and Patrick Surtain. Those guys can really cover. But when we play them, we want to make sure they also can tackle. We make them play football. We just don't want them to think they can concentrate all day on just trying to stop our receivers. We can get some matchups we want on offense, with play action and the threat of a run. We move our receivers around and try to create tough matchup problems for them. We were successful doing that in this game.

I'm encouraged by the way Lucas is coming along. We're starting to see some tangible things from him. We knew he had the intangibles—the desire to play and the commitment to trying to be a great quarterback. He is starting to get very comfortable, and he just might be a good quarterback in this league. He certainly has moved from a three to a two. Before the end of this season, I hope he will become a very good two.

There are a lot of first-year quarterbacks in the league this year. Kurt Warner, the kid in St. Louis, is having a Super Bowl year and has the best ratings of any quarterback in the league. But Ray now has better numbers than the rest. I mean guys like Tim Couch, Donovan McNabb, Akili Smith, Cade McNown, all of these kids who were drafted high this year.

This week he'll have a bit of a different test. We go to Dallas, and they play a little older style of defense. When they blitz, they play man-to-man, because they've got Deion Sanders and Kevin Smith at the corners. These two guys, if they're healthy, can really cover. Most teams are using the zone blitz, where they blitz and fall back into a zone. Dallas blitzes, and you get man-to-man behind it.

It will be imperative for Ray this week to make quick decisions and get rid of the ball. The coverage will be man-to-man. Our receivers just won't be able to find a hole in the zone defense and have Ray throw the ball to that hole. They'll be covered, and he will have to be quick getting the ball out and very accurate.

Ray can handle about 75 percent of our offense now. Vinny could handle 100 percent if he was playing. But Ray started with about one-third of it, and we've been expanding what he can do each week, and as he gets more comfortable, we have more confidence in him.

The best thing you can do as a coach is try to tailor your

game plan to the skills of the quarterback. They're all different. We had a different one for Simms and Hostetler with the Giants, and Bledsoe and Zolak with New England. Miami had a different one for Marino and Damon Huard. All guys are a little bit different, and you try to maximize their strengths. Ray is a good quarterback on the move. Vinny is better in the pocket. Ray can sprint out, he can bootleg, and do things Vinny can't do. Vinny can sprint out a little, bootleg a little, but those are not the things he can do best. With Ray, we have done a lot of that and it has been effective.

We've beat Miami three straight. We've done a good job handling Dan. We know he can't run and escape anymore, so we are not concerned with the outside, like you would have to be with a guy that can move, a guy like Flutie for example. So we rush all four men in the usual passing lanes, to take away those lanes. Dan is at his best when he moves up straight ahead and throws. He likes to step into the ball. If we collapse the pocket in front of him, it makes it harder for him to do this. It also gives us a better chance of getting a hand on the ball and deflecting it, and knocking it down.

But I think age is catching up to Dan. These older guys are hit and miss when you have to play them. We let Eric Green go. He's on injured reserve, but when the season is over we're going to cut the cord. It was a bad choice for us. He didn't help us, and we still owe him some money. I'm afraid the same thing is happening to Jumbo Elliott. He's been fighting a back problem for years, and he's not the same player he used to be. We picked up Steve Atwater, another older guy, in free agency, and he has been nicked. But he has helped us. When you go for an older guy you take a gamble. Tom Tupa, Vinny, Bryan Cox have turned out very well for us. Green did not. If I'm back here next year, I'll look a lot closer at any veterans we are thinking about bringing in here.

In fact, if I stay I'm going to review our whole injury situation. I've been very lucky as a coach. It's taken fifteen years for me to have a season like this in terms of injuries. But since it's happened, I'm going to review everything we have done. Vinny and Cascadden got serious leg injuries without being hit. Chrebet went out for almost half the season with a leg injury without being hit. Leon Johnson went out for the season, the first half of the first game, with a bad knee. Ferguson went out the same game, and missed three or four.

Beyond the injuries, there is a secondary factor here. Your training room becomes like a hospital ward. All of these injured guys are in there getting treated, and it becomes like a big social club. The injured guys are wondering what I'm thinking about. Do I want them anymore? Will they be back? The healthy guys look at the injured guys and start thinking that they might get injured and their careers could be in jeopardy.

It's not a healthy situation for a team. I try to cut off some of this stuff by spending time in there. I keep up with the injured guys. I talk to all of them to show them I do have an interest. I tell the healthy guys to get their asses out of there.

I've always believed, and it's worked well for me until this season, if you train them for strength, stamina, and endurance, you will have good results. In camp, we had only one injury. Otis Smith broke his shoulder hitting the ground. It wasn't a case of not working hard or not being in top shape. Because Otis was.

But for now, we have to play Dallas. I'd like to get on a little run here at the end of the year, and finish on a strong note.

DECEMBER 23, 1999

I thought I had seen everything there is to see in this game over the last twenty years, but I saw something in Dallas before we played the Cowboys last Sunday that was a first, and also disturbing.

I like to come out on the field, especially on the road, about two hours before the game and sort of look around. In most stadiums I'm looking at the wind and trying to judge what kind of impact it could have on the game. Or the sun, and when it might be a factor in the game, getting into the eyes of someone trying to catch the ball. A receiver. A kick returner. I also look for spots on the field, if it's grass, that might be slick or muddy, a potential problem.

You don't have to worry about most of that stuff in Dallas. The field is artificial, and most of Texas Stadium has a roof over it. Wind is never really a factor, but the sun can be, on a bright day. It sort of comes through the roof as a glare, where half of the field can be sunny, and the other half in shadow.

Well, as I start to walk around the field I look across and see the Dallas trainer and another guy working out some injured players. I see one of them is Larry Allen, who is the best offensive linemen in the league. He hasn't been playing for them the last couple of weeks, and I sure as hell hoped he wasn't going to be ready for us.

Boy Wonder, Curtis Martin, is my kind of running back.

But this is the thing that surprised and disturbed me. The other guy working out the injured players was Jerry Jones, the team owner. Now I've never seen that anywhere in my life, the owner working out injured players to see if they are ready to go or not. On most teams, one of the assistant coaches will work out the injured player, then they come back to the head coach and tell him what the deal is going to be. Whether that player can play or not.

Even though I've never had a lot to do with Jerry Jones, I like him as a person and respect him as an owner. He has always been very cordial to me whenever we've been around each other, which hasn't been too much, because I've never been big on going to league meetings. As a coach, I think they're a waste of time.

Jerry Jones, from what I was led to believe that day talking to some of the Dallas people, is very involved. I know at one time he played college ball and coached a kids team or something like that, but the NFL is supposed to be a little different. They tell me Jerry has a phone in his box that goes directly to the bench, and he'll call during the game with some message. Or if he wants to talk to certain players about their performance.

Hey, it's his team and he can do anything he wants with it. That's his prerogative. But I don't see any good it can do for him to get involved in the coaching end of the game. None whatsoever. I know he's a great marketing guy, maybe the best in the history of the league, and he knows how to make money with his team and his stadium.

If an owner wants to come around during the week and encourage the players, root for them, and let them know he is with them, that's fine with me. But once the owner wants to coach, then I'd be out of there the next day. I couldn't coach in that situation myself.

I wouldn't want to coach all week with my staff, getting the team ready the way we agreed we want them to get ready, and then have the owner step in on game day and start offering advice. That should not be his domain.

Jim Finks, who was a great general manager in this league and almost the commissioner after Pete Rozelle died, used to say: "Owners own. Managers manage. Coaches coach. Players play. That's the way it works best." Jim, who died a few years ago, was right. All of us have roles to play from top to bottom in every organization. If you hire a guy to do a job, then you should let the guy do the job.

More and more I see owners in this league who want to call attention to themselves, or are in it a few years and think they know more about football than guys who have been coaching most of their adult lives.

One of the first times I ever saw an owner down on the sidelines was Tom Benson doing some dizzy dance on the field after the Saints won a game. If he wants to do that, it's fine as far as I can see, because he isn't interfering with what is best for his coaches and his players. I wouldn't want any owner that I coached for dancing around the sideline, but if it makes him happy, good luck to him.

Years ago you could watch games on TV and never see the owner. There was no focus on the owner's box. Now you see it every game. I don't know why the people from the networks would think people are interested in seeing owners watching games. We don't see it, as far as I can see, in basketball or hockey, or baseball, during the regular season. You see it in the playoffs and World Series in baseball, because the owners like George Steinbrenner and Ted Turner usually come down and sit in a box close to the field.

I've been asked during this week what I thought about Orlando Brown knocking down the referee on purpose last Sunday. I didn't see it live, but I saw what happened later on the highlights. The referee, standing behind the play, threw a flag calling a penalty and it hit Brown, a big offensive lineman for Cleveland, in the eye. Brown then shoved the referee to the ground and got thrown out of the game. No decision has been made yet, but I hope they suspend him. You can't let the players start pushing officials around. There is no place for that in our game. If you do, if Tagliabue doesn't come down hard on this guy, then you will see some of these other guys trying to do the same thing.

Players are copycats. They see some player doing something in a game, and then it gets on *SportsCenter,* and they want to get the same attention for themselves, so they do it. It was like this throat-slashing gesture they just banned. One guy does it, and they all take a shot at it. It goes back to basketball and guys like Dennis Rodman. Those kinds of guys get attention, and the other guys think this is the way to become noticed.

Some people think Keyshawn is like that, but I really don't think he is. He likes to talk, but I think it is genuine. His personality is naturally exuberant. He's an "up" kind of person. He likes to play to the crowd, but I don't think he overdoes it. And when he is on the field, he backs up whatever he has to say. This kid loves to play football. He can't wait to get to the stadium. He always practices hard. He wants to learn. But when you are a marquee player, there are always guys that are not going to like you. He's had a great year for us. Caught over eighty balls and earned himself about $500,000 in incentives, and is going to the Pro Bowl for a second time.

Keyshawn wants in on the action. When he is on the field, he wants the ball. If you want him to block a linebacker, he'll block a linebacker. Most wideouts don't want much to do with blocking linebackers. He'll take it on. He'll catch the ball over the middle in traffic. Many guys shy away from that if they can. He's a strong, physical guy. If you put him on defense, he'll tackle somebody. If you want him to block a punt, he'd do that also. Keyshawn is a football player first. He might not come across that way, but that's what he is. He's not afraid. He has great confidence in himself. He thinks he can dominate anyone. They made a big deal about his matchup with Deion Sanders in this game, but it didn't happen too much. Keyshawn caught six passes, but I don't know on how many of those he was up against Deion.

We beat Dallas 22–21 by getting ahead late in the game on a field goal and then stopping Dallas when they tried to come back. It was a big win for us. Our players were very happy, and they deserved to be. Dallas is not the Dallas of old, and they won't be for a long time. But they were still pretty good, playing in their own building with the playoffs on the line.

Many of our guys had never played in that building before, and it is different. There are some pregame distractions in Dallas that don't occur anywhere else. It's the only place where hundreds of people are walking around the perimeter of the field when the team is warming up. Jones gives fans this perk for buying an expensive seat. He has them taken down on the field so they can have the experience of being there just before the game. When the Dallas players come up by position to practice, let's say all of the linebackers in a group, they blow horns and shoot off rockets. If you don't expect it, or know what it is, you can get distracted by it.

I was very worried toward the end of the third period. They scored a touchdown and went up by eight. I was pissed off at our defense. They gave it up on a long drive. I didn't like the looks of it. When they came to the sideline I went over to talk to the defensive players, and told them if they didn't pick it up and make some plays, the game was going to be out of reach for us. Luckily, we came right back on offense and scored a touchdown, but we missed the extra points when we tried for two, looking to tie the game. Ray Lucas misread the play. It was supposed to be a quarterback draw, and we didn't run it right.

Then later, in the fourth period, we had miscommunication between Ray and our center, Kevin Mawae, which resulted in a fumble that Dallas recovered. We snapped the ball on the wrong count, and Ray fumbled the ball. It looked bad, but then our defense stepped up and made the critical play. We intercepted a pass with about five minutes to play.

Troy Aikman wasn't in great shape. At times he looked like he was disinterested. He's always been a quarterback that seems to be nonchalant about what he is doing, even when they were winning Super Bowls. But for some reason, he just didn't seem to be on top of his game. Of course, he doesn't have the great cast around him that he had when they won the three Super Bowls.

Jay Novacek is gone at tight end, and he was the guy that Aikman looked to when he was in trouble. The guys they have now can't do what Novacek did for him. Michael Irvin didn't play and is probably finished. He was a very consistent player. Aikman had great trust in him. They had Daryl "Moose" Johnston at fullback, and he's gone. So all of the guys he played so well with, with the exception of Emmitt Smith, are not there.

Emmitt is amazing. I've got a lot of respect for him. He's tough. He's smart. He's a great downhill runner. His secret is that he runs into the hole before he makes his cuts. You can count the number of guys who can do that on one hand. The rest of them start their cut in the backfield. They don't have faith in the play. All of them should watch Emmitt. I'm still on Curtis Martin a lot about that, cutting before he gets to the hole. He still does it, but not as much as he used to. I told Curtis over the years to watch Emmitt, and watch what he does—how Emmitt trusts the play.

We kicked a field goal to get the lead with under two minutes to play, and they had a chance to go back down and get a score to beat us. We were ahead by just two points, and a field goal would have done it. But we stopped them on downs, and took over to win the game.

Defensively, Dallas is still pretty good. Deion is a great player, but he's getting older and not quite what he was a few years back. He's also getting hurt more than he did before. Deion doesn't like to tackle. He will if you force him to, but he doesn't go around looking for someone to hit. You don't want to throw to the sideline when he is in coverage. You're inviting a lot of trouble if you do. He looks for that pass. Inside, he isn't as good. You can beat him inside.

We felt like we had to block their blitz. Dallas likes to attack on defense. They'll blitz a lot, send a lot of guys. But they do it more with man-to-man coverage behind the blitzers than zones, like most other teams are doing. They like to rush seven, and cover tight with the other four. We had to mix the run with the pass.

Curtis played well. We ran for about 125 yards. Not great, but it made them respect our running game and gave us a chance to attack them downfield with play action. We also wanted to slow down their linebackers. They are not big, but they are very fast. So we made sure we had someone chipping those guys, to slow them down, and this helped in our success.

Curtis finished as first alternate in the Pro Bowl voting, but he deserves being on the team. I don't wish any bad luck for the guys voted in front of him, but I'd like to see him make the trip and play in the game.

We call Curtis "Boy Wonder." It's a nickname I gave to him in New England. He's a wonderful football player. No one is more dedicated. This kid will be in here for eleven hours today. Eleven hours. He'll be one of the first in, and the last out. You don't ever have to worry about Curtis. He is a model for clean living. He is truly a dedicated player. This is his profession, and he approaches it that way. His life is built around his job. He is in tremendous shape. He comes in here to work out when he doesn't have to work out. Everyone else is gone, and he comes back. He lifts weights. He'll go in the hot tub, the cold pool, and leave nothing to chance. When he leaves here, he gets something to eat, and then goes home for the night. He's a spartan warrior. That's why I wanted to get him so badly from New England when he was available. I don't know of anyone else like him in the league.

We've got Miami again. They'll be tough. They always are at home. We played them just two weeks ago, so this will be a period of adjustment. They'll look at what we did well against them and try to take that away from us. We'll do the same to them. But this late in the season, you can only do so much. It all comes back to what your team can do consistently well. We've beaten them three in a row. Our kids usually get ready to play Miami, and that's because Miami has been the team to beat for so long in this division.

I'm anxious to get another look at Marino. He didn't have his best when we played them two weeks ago. Maybe he'll pick it up playing in warmer weather. This could be his last home game. If we beat them, they might get knocked out of the play-offs, and if they do make it, they'll be a wild card and won't play at home. I'm sure he'll have that in the back of his mind and will want to come up with a big game.

Jimmy Johnson and I talking before our last game against each other.

DECEMBER 30, 1999

We just had our best win of the season, and I'm feeling good about our chances of finishing upbeat, which, about six weeks ago, I wouldn't have given much chance of happening.

We beat Miami down there on Monday night in a very tough football game. No one on either side had anything left in their tank when this one was over. They were throwing their best shots all night. We took them, and then, in the end, we finished off the Dolphins by playing big in the fourth quarter.

Now we've got a short week to get ready for Seattle. They're coming in here Sunday needing to win. They've got the playoffs and the division on the line. We didn't get home from Miami until early Tuesday morning, and this is Christmas week. I've got to keep these guys on track and it isn't going to be easy. There are a lot of distractions: the holidays, pressure from the family. Our ownership situation seems to be close at hand, but not close enough for me. I wanted this thing over and done with by December 15, and I was told that was going to happen. Now it's not, and I've got a decision to make about what I want to do. I think I know the answer. In fact, I'm about 90 percent sure at this point. But I'd like to talk it over with the next owner to see where he is coming from and his response to what I would like to do.

A couple of weeks ago we beat Miami in New York. When you play games against the same team so close together there are important periods of adjustment by both coaching staffs. You can change some things most of the time, but not a lot. Or at least that's what we thought.

Miami caught us by surprise with their offense and had us on our heels defensively the whole night. Our defense was bad, but theirs wasn't that good either. They moved the ball consistently the entire game until the fourth period. But we made the bigger plays in the game, and that is why we won.

I thought we had a good chance to win going into the game, but I also knew Miami has a very hostile atmosphere during those night games down there. Those people really get pumped up. We beat them in a very close game last year on a Sunday night by making big plays in the fourth quarter.

Before the game, I told my team: "This is a team you've had success against. You beat them three in a row. This gives you an edge. You know you can beat them. They don't know that they can beat you. Now we need to prove it to them one more time that we can beat them. That we've got their number. It might be tougher this time, because they've got the playoffs on the line, but we can do it."

Miami changed their attack on offense. During the season, no matter what, they ran the ball. Jimmy Johnson's been saying all year that they were going to keep running, even when their running game wasn't any good. In this game, they didn't even try to run.

Right from the start they came out throwing, and threw the entire night. And they also did some nice things in their offensive blocking schemes to make it worse for us. Like I said a couple of chapters before, in recent years we've been attacking Dan Marino up the middle. We try to take away the usual passing lanes. We try to have guys coming right in his face. We don't even worry about him running out of the pocket, or trying to get to the outside to throw. He can't move anymore. He knows it. We know it. But Miami's coaches made a nice adjustment. They sealed everything off, from the outside in, and made it impossible to get pressure on him from the inside. We also realize that Dan is better, and more effective, when he steps up in the pocket and gets his body into the throw.

By the way, he threw a lot better in this game than he did a couple of weeks ago here in New York. In that one, he didn't have much on the ball. It was sort of hanging when he threw it. In this game, he had his old zip back. Not quite to where it was at his peak, but still enough to play a fine game. He threw better because we couldn't crack the pocket in front of him to prevent him from stepping up. They made it comfortable for him to throw. The other times we've played him the last couple of years, we always made it uncomfortable for him by jamming people into the middle, right in his face.

The game was a back-and-forth battle with both offenses moving the ball. They even used some of our own offensive stuff against us. One time they ran a bunch formation, which is what we like to do, and caught us with our pants down. A kid named J. J. Johnson ran thirty yards for a touchdown on a sweep, while the guys in our secondary were still talking about who they were supposed to cover in man-to-man, and we got run over.

Neither team had control of the game. I never felt that we did until the last couple of minutes. We had two good drives at the beginning of the game. Ray Lucas played his best game in this one, and he's playing better every game. He's fun to watch and coach.

There were six or seven plays that turned the game for us. We were up 10–7, and they looked like they were going in for a touchdown. They were moving the ball easily on us. Our secondary couldn't cover anyone.

Marino threw two interceptions that really hurt them and got us a couple of scores. Marcus Coleman made a great play to intercept a Marino pass and run it back ninety-something yards for a touchdown. He played it perfectly. We knew one of the plays their offense likes to run close to the goal line. It is what we call a slant/cut. The receiver starts to slant toward the middle of the field, and between five and ten yards deep, makes a quick cut to the inside. Two things happened to make the play for us. First, Coleman guessed right. He saw what was happening, closed fast to the inside of the field, and cut under the receiver. At the same time, because we weren't getting any pressure inside, we blitzed a guy from the outside, and forced Dan to get rid of the ball before he wanted to. But I think Dan still felt he would be safe to make the throw until Coleman cut in front of the receiver, made the catch, and ran it all the way back for a score to put us in the lead, 17–7.

In the second half, we had Marino backed up against his own goal line in a passing situation, and we brought some pressure from the outside. He saw it coming and tried to dump the ball off. Roman Phifer stepped in front of the receiver to make the interception, which set up the score for us inside their five-yard line.

In spite of those two throws, Marino played a good game against us. He threw for something like 320 yards, and that doesn't happen very often. Defensively, he never let us get in any rhythm. They spread our defense out with their formations and attacked us. Our defensive coaches were under a lot of stress. I could see that. In a situation like that, I don't step in because that would only create more stress. All of us knew what was going on, we just couldn't figure out what to do about it. The good thing is that we did make two big defensive plays to get us fourteen points.

We had four very key plays on offense in the second half. On a third and short, we thought they would blitz us, and we called a pass to Wayne Chrebet. We didn't block it the way we should have. Zach Thomas broke loose quickly and was closing in on Lucas. Ray had to hold the ball and take a hit to give Chrebet the time to make his move to beat Patrick Surtain, a pretty good cover guy, in a man-to-man situation. Ray laid the ball out there, and Chrebet ran under it to give us a long touchdown. They thought they were going to stop us and get the ball back.

On the next possession, we stopped them again when they tried for a long field goal to tie the game. We were up 24–21, and Jimmy went for a fifty-four yarder. This became a critical call for them in the game. I knew what Jimmy was thinking. Even though it was long, you could tell from where we were down on the field that their kicker, Orlindo Mare, had some wind at his back. He kicked it long enough, but he kicked it wide.

We were still up by three and had good field position, because the ball went back to where he missed the kick. During the television time-out, we talked about what we were going to do. I thought Miami would think we were going to run the ball, take time off the clock, and try to win with the three points.

We were running the ball well on them all night. Curtis Martin was having another very impressive game. In particular, we had been very successful on this one play, which entailed bringing him in motion and then running the ball.

We had designed a pass play off that running play for just such an occasion. We had Lucas run the same play but fake it to Curtis on play action, and then look for Dedric Ward deep. He's our fastest receiver. We thought with the formation we had called, he could beat Terrell Buckley, the slowest of their three primary cover guys in man-to-man situations. That's the way it worked out. Ray made a nice fake to Curtis. Buckley paused for a second, thinking run, and then Ward blew right past him to catch a perfectly thrown ball for another touchdown. I called it "going for the throat." And I was told later by a friend that Scott Zolak, one of my former players, was yelling from their sideline, "He's going for the throat! He's going for the throat!"

But Miami's defense didn't know what the hell he was talking about. Scott told friends that as soon as he saw the formation, and the situation, he knew we were going to throw deep. A year before, when he was playing in New England, we had a similar situation. We had a small lead, got the ball back on first down, and hit Ward with a bomb over a kid named Chris Canty, for a long score that put the game out of reach.

We were up by ten, 31–21, but I still wasn't comfortable when we got the ball back. Dan Marino still can be Dan Marino. He's won just about as many games as any quarterback in the history of the game, taking his team up and down the field in the closing minutes to score points.

You can be up by ten with the clock on your side, but you still are paranoid. Part of you is thinking about moving the ball and not giving it back to them. The other part is thinking they might get it back, score a quick touchdown, get an onside kick, and score again to beat you.

We got the ball back with a couple of minutes left, but they were using up their time-outs to stop the clock. We had a fourth down and short just over midfield, when we called a time-out. Our staff had some options to talk about.

I was going back and forth with my offensive coaches upstairs, Charlie Weis and Dan Henning. We talked about punting, but if the ball went into the end zone, we wouldn't gain that much. We talked about kicking a long field goal. Our guy has a leg as strong as anyone in the league, but to me, it was a low-percentage play and a high risk. Then we talked about running the ball for a first down, but we felt their defense would gang up the line of scrimmage against the run, figuring we wouldn't gamble on throwing it, and risk an interception.

So we took that gamble. Let's throw a short, but safe, pass, to get us the first down. We had three plays in the game plan for this situation. We picked the one we liked best. Ray takes a quick roll to his right and hits Keyshawn Johnson on a quick throw. Ray did it perfectly. Got rid of the ball quick and on target.

But Keyshawn gave us a scare. He's got great hands, but he nearly dropped this one. He double caught it. He caught it, popped it in the air, and then caught it again for the first down and the game.

I was elated when we won but also a little sad. I like Jimmy Johnson. I liked competing against him, all the way back to when he came into the league with Dallas and I was coaching the Giants. He's a helluva coach. But the feeling I got from talking with him the last couple of weeks is that he's had it, and this will be his last year coaching. He was down on his players and seemed to be fed up with the situation.

And then there's Marino. What a tough son of a bitch. What a competitor. He scared the heart out of every coach that he has ever gone up against. When I've coached, there were only a few that could do that—Elway, Cunningham, and to a lesser degree Jim Kelly. These were mobile quarterbacks who bring sleepless nights. They kill you with improvisation. Give me a guy any day that just stands in the pocket and throws.

I don't think Dan and I will ever be competing on the same field again. It could be me leaving, or him. But I don't think it will happen again.

After the game I told my kids in the locker room how proud I was of them and the way they sucked it up and hung in there through a lot of adversity. I told them it was a hell of a win, but to wait until next week to enjoy it. We didn't have the time to do it now.

We didn't take off from Miami until 2:15 in the morning and didn't get back to New York until 4:30. After waiting for luggage, we didn't get back to the offices until 5:30. The coaches didn't go home, and we didn't go to sleep. I told the players I didn't want to see them until noon Wednesday. I changed the schedule to accommodate the time we were losing to the Monday night game next week. I'm just going to try to cram everything into Thursday and Friday, more than I normally would. I think we had a good feel for what we have to do. We beat Seattle in New York last year, so our players are familiar with them.

Because Friday is the new millennium, and everyone is wondering what is going to happen with the Y2K stuff, Seattle will come to town on Friday. The league has mandated that the traveling teams this weekend be in town forty-eight hours before kickoff, instead of the usual twenty-four hours. The league is worried about airlines being shut down, or travel being curtailed, and they don't want to take any chances. So I know their players are going to be in town, but I told my guys I didn't want a lot of socializing.

I told our players to stay in and rest. I don't care what their wives want them to do on New Year's Eve. Stay in. Celebrate next week. You've got all off-season to celebrate. I talked to them hard about that. About paying attention to business, and I think they will.

JANUARY 6, 2000

I'm not going to coach here anymore, but what we thought was going to happen here is not going to happen. Bill Belichick, who was supposed to be our next head coach, walked out on us. Belichick had a contract with the New York Jets that said he is the next coach after I step down. He even accepted a $1 million bonus from Mr. Hess last year to stay around to take the job. I'm not sure how all of this is going to turn out.

Maybe the best way to handle this issue is to explain the recent chain of events, which began last Friday. On Friday, two days before the last Jets game, I made my decision not to coach again. I had been thinking that way for weeks but really didn't know for sure until we finished practice.

We worked indoors in our bubble, and when I was walking off the field, something inside me made me stop and look around. And then a voice inside me said, "This is your last practice as a coach."

It just happened. My mind, my body, whatever. Something inside just said, "This is it." We practice on Saturdays, but to a coach, Saturday isn't really practice. You sort of just loosen up and go over some odds and ends. As I walked back to my office, I felt a sense of relief. But I didn't tell anyone, not even my wife. It wasn't 100 percent definite, because part of me wanted to go

Bill Belichick and I roamed the sidelines for many years together. When I retired as coach, I was hoping he would step up and take my place.

out winning a game. But I was very confident we were going to beat Seattle.

The players were prepared. I looked at every one of them Saturday morning, and not one of them looked tired or hung over after New Year's Eve. We beat Seattle, 19–9, but the game wasn't even that close. We could have, and probably should have, scored at least thirty points, but after we struggled at the beginning, I felt like we were in control of the game in the second half.

Mike Holmgren is one of the best coaches in the game. When you play him or one of his teams, whether in Green Bay or Seattle, it's a chess match. He has a great knack for substituting his players. He loves to conceal what he is going to do. He changes what he does game by game with his personnel substitutions. His pattern can be erratic, and defensively, you just have to hang with him because sooner or later you will discover just what he's is trying to do. When you're coaching against him, you hope it's sooner rather than later.

In this game, we shut them down in the second half, and they couldn't convert against our defense. We won because we controlled the ball and the clock with our running game. That's what I have loved to do my whole coaching career, so I thought it was kind of fitting that my last game happened the way it did.

Curtis Martin was magnificent. I'm really going to miss being around that kid. He is truly "Boy Wonder." If they were all like him, no one would ever quit coaching. He ran for 158 yards. His total offense this year was among the best in the league. He has 6,300 yards for his five-year career, so he has averaged better than 1,200 per season. I'm not saying he is the best in the league, but I mean this with all my heart: I'll take him over any back in the league, and you can have the rest.

What really helped us is that we got ahead early. Ricky Watters is a good back, but he can't run the ball if they don't give it to him. He had only thirty-three yards rushing on the day, because they had to go away from the run and start throwing to catch up.

I was happy for myself and my team and all Jets fans when it was over.

To think we were 1 and 6 at one point, and then came all the way back to 8 and 8, beating a bunch of playoff teams (Miami, Seattle, Dallas, Buffalo) at the end of the season, made me very proud.

I had told them at midseason, when things looked the worst, "It's too soon to quit." Those were my exact words. I told them there was a way out, if they believed in it and worked to find it.

And they did.

Of course, I thought about some of those games we gave away early in the season that we should have won, and started thinking about what would happen this weekend if we were in the playoffs. The way we finished, I don't think any team would be looking forward to playing us.

Saturday after practice, I called in Belichick and told him I was pretty sure I was going to retire after the game. I told him, "By contract, you're the next head coach." I asked him if he still wanted to be the Jets head coach.

"I've been waiting a year for this," he said. I told him that Sunday after the game, I was going to inform Steve Gutman of my decision. I told Belichick, "As soon as I do that, you're the head coach, and I plan to do it right after the game." And I did. It was all very matter of fact, and Bill didn't seem that excited about it. If this is what he had been waiting to hear for a year, he should have been more exuberant. But he wasn't. I didn't think anything of it at the time.

I told Steve and asked him to tell John Hess, which he did.

As for why I decided to retire, I go back to a meeting of a year ago with Mr. Hess, Steve Gutman, and Belichick. I told Mr. Hess that, win or lose, I thought it was going to be my last year coaching, but I wanted to leave the window of opportunity open to return to coach another year, if I decided to do so.

But deep down, even then, I felt that this would be my last season.

When I first came to the Jets, Mr. Hess said, "You can coach one, two, three years, however long you want to coach."

We put four years in the contract.

Then he said to me, "Four is just a number. When you step down from coaching you are going to be director of football operations if you want to be. But coach as long as you want."

After last year, we planned accordingly. Belichick was aware of that. In fact, during the last season, I had a lot of meetings with him, sort of preparing him to take over this season, things I would not have shared with him in the past. Even before the season started, I had heard rumors that New England was interested in Belichick.

There was even a story in the *Boston Herald* that quoted a Patriots source as saying Belichick would be the next head coach of the Patriots if they fired Pete Carroll.

The year before, when the season was over, Kansas City and Chicago were interested in Bill as head coach and requested permission to speak with him. But he turned them down. Mr. Hess had given him a $1 million bonus just to stay around and be the next head coach, and for bypassing any offers that might come his way to go somewhere else.

Then late in this past season, I started to hear some more rumors, nothing substantiated, about Belichick going to the Patriots. There were no coaching vacancies at the time, and the league has a rule that a team cannot call and ask permission to talk to a coach until the season is over.

At 9:00 in the morning, the day after the season, just before I was going to announce my intention to retire, first to my staff and later to my players, we got a fax in the Jets' office from New England, requesting permission to speak with Belichick about being head coach and general manager of the Patriots.

We rejected permission, saying he had been head coach of the Jets since 5:00 P.M., the night before, when I officially resigned as head coach to Steve Gutman.

I had the meeting with my coaches. I told them I was leaving and that by contract, Bill Belichick was now head coach. I walked out of the meeting, and from what I learned from the assistant coaches in the meeting with Belichick, he acted like he was the new head coach, and set up a full staff meeting for Tuesday morning the next day.

Steve Gutman and I sat in a meeting with Belichick that day with our trainer to talk about the injured players. I know he spoke that day with Scott Pioli, our director of pro personnel, about preparing for free agency.

And I know he spoke with Mike Tannenbaum, who runs our salary cap, about getting together with him later in the week.

Monday evening was the first time I saw any reluctance, or hesitation, on the part of Belichick. It was about 6:00 in the evening. I was in the coaches locker area, and he came in. He had heard about the offer from the Patriots and wanted to talk to them about it.

I was surprised. I told him I denied them permission. I told him he told me Saturday that he had been waiting a year to get the job. I told him he was the head coach of the Jets.

He said things had changed since the time Mr. Hess died, and he didn't know who the next owner was going to be, or how he was going to react to the situation. I told him that if this is the way he was thinking, he better rethink whether or not he wanted to be the head coach of the Jets, and that I wasn't giving permission for New England to talk with him.

He tried to tell me that after eighteen years of being with me, he felt I owed him that opportunity to go coach in New England if that is what he wanted to do. I wasn't going to do that.

I told him he had the contract with the Jets, and he was given a lot of money from Mr. Hess to be the Jets head coach, and that I owed it to the franchise to see that either he was the head coach, or that we got compensated for his services if he left.

When he left, I thought it was just a conversation with a guy trying to review all his options, and nothing more. I thought he was still going to want to coach the Jets.

In retrospect, I think something happened with Belichick or with his agent, on Monday afternoon that made Belichick reconsider his position with the Jets.

I can't prove it, and I really don't care now that he has quit.

From what I learned later, Belichick was not the same guy on Tuesday that he was on Monday. He was visibly nervous. He couldn't stop his hands from shaking in the coaches meeting, which he called to an early halt, and he told his staff that he would get back to them later.

On Tuesday, when I came back from taping my weekly television show with Phil Simms, I sat in my office at about 2:15 or 2:20. I was told Belichick had a press conference scheduled for 2:30 to talk about being the head coach of the Jets. He said he didn't want to have one on Monday because he considered it my day with the media.

Less than ten minutes before he was to speak, he stopped in my office and said he was going to resign. I wasn't shocked, but I was still surprised. He didn't say much, only that things had changed since Mr. Hess had died. He said he wanted to quit, and I told him if that's what you want to do, then go ahead and do it. I also told him that we weren't giving permission to New England to interview him for their vacant head coaching job, and as far as I was concerned, he was out of coaching for three years, unless something changed.

Then he went down the hall and had the weird press conference. He was just too emotional to handle the situation. And he said some things about me that weren't true. He also said some things that were said in private conversations between coaches, which coaches know are not to be repeated.

He was obviously under a lot of stress, and it isn't going to get any better because he is under contract with us and he's not going to coach anywhere unless we let him. His excuse about things changing with the death of Mr. Hess was weak.

Mr. Hess had been dead for seven months. The potential buyers of the Jets were all told by Goldman Sachs that Belichick, by contract, would automatically be the next coach as soon as I stepped down, if I decided to step down. They were told my retirement was a possibility.

When Belichick's press conference was over Tuesday, most of us just felt sad for what we just saw. I spoke with Steve Gutman, who stood at the press conference, and after watching it and hearing it he felt that Belichick "was in personal turmoil."

We informed the league of what had just happened and sent them all of the contracts and papers regarding Belichick that we had on file. Gutman was very upset by what just happened, but he knew that Belichick's contract was legal and binding, and felt the commissioner would say the same thing.

The next day, yesterday, he did. He sent a fax around the league to every team, telling them not to speak with Belichick about a job, because he was under contract to us.

When Belichick left, I told Steve I wasn't going to abandon the franchise. I told him to call John Hess and tell him that we were going to keep the ship on course. I had invested too much blood and sweat in this organization the past three years to let this thing fall apart.

Gutman told me he thinks Belichick and his agent, Neil Cornrich, will file some kind of action with Tagliabue before the week is over. Since this happened, the newspapers are speculating that I will come back to coach.

I will not coach again. I have told Steve Gutman that. I have not changed my mind, no matter what they are writing, and I won't change my mind.

And here's why.

The dressing room was ecstatic after we beat Seattle. They didn't know I was quitting. They might have had an idea, because during the week some of them had told me they hoped I would come back, so we could take a run at the championship next year.

But in the locker room Sunday they were happy, excited, and unified. They were proud. You could not hear a sound when I told them this:

"This ought to be an indication to you that you never, never,

never, give up. It took twenty-three weeks, but you finally dug yourselves out of the hole. You are on level ground again. Let this season serve you well for the future, no matter what you do."

Ray Lucas hugged me and thanked me. He told me I had faith in him when no one else did. I told him he earned that faith and respect. I had a chance to speak to just a couple of more players on the way out the door to the press conference, but when I came back, most of them were gone.

But I knew I had the chance to tell all of them Monday morning how I felt about them, and what I was going to do. I scheduled a meeting for 9:30 in the morning.

I felt I had to tell them face-to-face what I was feeling so they would understand. This is what I told them:

Since I've been here coaching you, I've told all of you there is no shame in leaving this game when your time has come. I told you that if someday you were in the weight room, and you decided that you never wanted to lift another weight in your life, there was no shame in that. I told you if you were on the field, and you made up your mind that you just didn't feel like hitting anyone anymore, then there was no shame in that. And when I tell you this morning that I do not want to coach anymore, I feel no shame. It is time for me to go. I could stand up here and tell you, I can coach sixteen more games. Or thirty-two more games. Or even forty-eight more games. I know I could do that. But I know I cannot do it with the same commitment I have done it in the past. The same commitment I ask you to give me as players: a total commitment.

During the season, in one of our weekly conversations with my friend Ron Wolf of the Green Bay Packers, somehow the poem "The Guy in the Glass" by Dale Wimbrow came up, and I told him I had heard of it, and asked him to send me a copy.

He faxed it over a few minutes later, and I kept it in my desk. I read it that morning to the players.

It was very emotional.

I had a hard time reading the last few lines, but I got through it.

The poem is about being able to look at yourself, and knowing who you are, and what you are. What others say and think about you is not as important as what you can say, and feel, about yourself.

I was telling them, through this poem, that life is about being true to yourself, and that in the end, if you are not happy with the man you see in the mirror, in the glass, you are going to go through the rest of your life experiencing a lot of heartache.

When I finished no one said a word. I could feel the silence as I walked out of the room. I could also feel the love from the players.

I was crying, but I didn't feel any shame about that either.

FEBRUARY 9, 2000

The season has been over for more than a month, and a lot has happened. I'm in Jupiter, Florida, sitting in one of my homes and trying to recall, as best I can, the events that brought Woody Johnson in as our new owner, that sent Bill Belichick on his way to New England as the Patriots head coach, that made Al Groh the head coach of the Jets, and have me sitting here today thinking about what I'm going to do with the rest of my life.

I know this much. I did the right thing. With each day that goes by, I know I don't want to coach anymore. I'm very comfortable with that.

I also don't know what I want to do in the future. I did tell Woody Johnson that I would stay active with the team for the next six months, trying to help with free agency, the draft, mini-camp, and anything I can do right up to training camp in July.

After that, I'm not sure. Part of me wants to get away from pro football completely, but I'm not sure I want to go that far yet. I think television is a possibility. Or going into private business. I feel like I want to do all of the things I've never done in my life before. All of the things I couldn't do because of football. Whatever I do, I'm going to leave plenty of time to just take it easy and enjoy myself.

Woody Johnson has been great. I think he will be very good for the Jets, our fans, the NFL, and sports in general. He's a

Al Groh, the new head coach of the Jets, will do great things for the organization.

sports fan. He has some good ideas. He also has an idea of what he wants for the Jets in the future.

I met with him briefly just after he bought the team for $635 million. Most of that conversation was about the Belichick situation, and possible legal action. The next time we met, we talked for a couple of hours, and almost all of it was about his vision of the Jets and what he wanted to do with the club in the future.

At that time, there was a lot of "creative" writing going on in New York. One story said Woody Johnson offered me $5 million to coach another year. That's not true, and Johnson addressed that when it came up at his press conference. A few more publications said they offered me $25 million to stay around another five years. Coach a year or two more, then move into the front office.

That never happened. Woody and I never talked about that. Not once. He did ask me if I would consider coming back to coach. I said no. I told Woody I had been coaching a long time and it was time to stop. I told him what I told the players—that I couldn't give it the commitment I had given it in the past, so I wasn't going to coach again. And Woody understood.

I did feel an obligation to the organization and said I would stay around to pick a new coach and deal with whatever was going to happen to Belichick. If we allowed Belichick to go to New England, the compensation would at least have to be a first-round draft choice in the year 2000. We agreed that we shouldn't make any deal with any team unless we got at least that.

Belichick went to court, and his case was basically thrown out. The next day he withdrew any case he had against the league or us. I thought about calling Bob Kraft to see if we could make a deal. I hadn't talked to Kraft since the day I left New England, and there had been a lot of hard feelings on both sides.

It wasn't easy for me to make the call.

But I wanted, deep down, to do it. I wanted to get what I called "the border war" over. I wanted to see if we could put the past behind us, and get on with the future. If we could do that, then we could see if we could come to an agreement on Belichick.

I called his office about 7:00 at night and told the secretary who was calling. I don't think she believed me, but Bob came on the phone. I told Bob it was "Darth Vader," and he started to laugh a little. I think that broke the ice.

He was very receptive to talking about what had gone on between us and trying to get it resolved. We both agreed that it would be better for both franchises and the National Football League if we did.

I told him that I did some things leaving New England that I would not have done if I had a chance to do it over again. He said if he knew then what he knew now as an owner, he would have done some things differently as well.

Once we got through that, we started talking about Belichick. I asked him, "Bob, do you want this guy to be your head coach?"

He said, "Yeah."

I said, "Okay, there's going to be some compensation involved."

He said he would offer a third-round draft pick this year and a fourth the next year.

I told him we weren't interested unless there was a first-round choice involved this year. He wanted to think about it, so we made an agreement to talk the next morning. He called and changed his offer to a second this year, and a third the next year.

I told him the same thing. "Bob, we are not going to make a deal, unless we get a first this year."

Again, our conversation was healthy, but he said he didn't want to give up a first for Belichick, and that he had decided he wanted to get going in another direction. When we hung up that day, it was amicable, but I felt there was not going to be a deal.

That night at about 11:00, Bob called back. I was surprised.

He said, "I'm going to make a decision here that I don't want to make, because I want this guy as my head coach."

I said, "We can work this out. Let's do this. You give me the one this year, and a four next year, then I give you back a five the next year.

"Then I would like to have a seventh round choice from you the year after that."

He said he'd go for the one and the four, and getting a five back was okay. But he would only put a seven in there if it was necessary, but he really didn't want to do that.

Bob told me to put down in writing what I thought was right, and send it to him by fax the next morning.

I called him and said I was sending him the letter with the seven in the deal, but that I would give him back a seven the next year after that. So that's the way it ended up. We got a first, fourth, and seventh. Bob got back a fifth and a seventh. We both thought that was fair.

Then he said he still had to get Belichick signed, and I told Bob I thought I could help him with that.

I suggested he tell Belichick that this deal had to be done in forty-eight hours, or there wasn't going to be any deal. I said to him, "Let's put a window in the deal. That way he can't leverage either team, trying to make his deal. It helps us. It helps you."

I then called Belichick and told him we had made a tentative deal to let him go to New England, but that he had to make his deal in less than forty-eight hours or it was off. He understood.

I think he was surprised by the call. I'm sure he thought he was dead in the water for three years and wouldn't be coaching. I mentioned that the deal still had to be finalized by the league with all of the paperwork signed off by both teams and the league office. I told him to stay by the phone. He didn't seem to think this deal was going to happen.

When the deal was finalized, I called Belichick back and told him he had permission to call Kraft. He said he appreciated what had just happened. I wished him luck. I didn't want to keep Belichick out of coaching. That wouldn't have served any purpose.

The best thing for everybody was to make the deal. We

deserved compensation because he will make New England better. He has already taken some of our Jets people with him. And he certainly has a great knowledge of how we are doing things as an organization.

Woody Johnson was with this thing all the way. He understood why we should hang in there to get a first-round choice.

As far as Belichick goes, we are even. I hired him as my defensive coordinator when I got the Giants head coaching job. I recommended him to Cleveland when he got that job. When they fired him in Cleveland, I picked him up in New England. I took him to the Jets with me and set him up to be the Jets head coach of the future.

Bill did a good job for me, but I did a good job for him. Honestly, I still can't figure out why he didn't take this job, instead of going to New England. If the Patriots never came forward, I think he would have been very happy to be the head coach of the New York Jets. Instead, Al Groh has been promoted from linebackers coach.

I think Al Groh will do a great job. When the Belichick thing was still up in the air I talked to Woody Johnson about the next head coach. We knew it wasn't going to be Belichick after he walked out on us. I wanted Al Groh because he knew the history of what we had done with the Jets the three previous seasons.

He knew what the team was like when we got there, he knew how we turned it around. Al knows what the players are like and how they expect to be coached. I told Mr. Johnson that I thought it was better if we took someone off our staff, rather than go outside. An outsider would most likely set back a lot of stuff that had been accomplished by winning thirty games in three years.

But before we moved to make Al the head coach, I wanted Woody to meet him so they could get a feel for each other. Woody was impressed with him. Bringing in Al was the best of all possible options we had.

I still don't know for sure when I will leave, but I don't think I'll be around a year from now. It will probably be sooner than that. I want to make sure Mr. Johnson knows what he needs to know about being an owner in the National Football League. I feel I owe that to Mr. Hess and the Jets.

Every time I left a job in this league, I felt I left a team in better shape than I found it. I feel that way about the Giants, about the Patriots, and now about the Jets. I wish my final season could have been better, but as I told my players the last time I met with them, there's no shame in leaving, when you know for sure it's time to go.

AFTERWORD

When I think about some of the things that happened in the last twelve months I have to laugh. If someone told me that we weren't even going to compete after all we put into getting ready for the 1999 season, I would have told them they were out of their minds. We spent all of the money we had to give it our best shot. But the injuries in the opening game were just too much to overcome, and the Belichick fiasco at the end of the season was beyond comprehension.

I've been thinking back a lot and recalling a conversation I had with Dick Vermiel last year. I don't know how many people know this, but the Rams were trying to get rid of him after the 1998 season. His team was 4 and 12, he was on a long-term contract, and the team wanted to buy him out and get another coach. Dick told them to make him an offer. They did, and he didn't take it. It wasn't enough. If they had given him a better deal, he would have been gone. Instead he stayed, coached the season, and won the Super Bowl with a quarterback no one wanted either. Not even the Rams. If they did, they would have never put Kurt Warner on the expansion list for the Cleveland Browns, who could have had him for nothing. But they didn't want him either. Then Warner had a great year and became the Most Valuable Player.

These are two great illustrations about why you can never count on anything in the NFL. We looked like a good thing and went nowhere. They looked like they had no chance and won it all. I was so happy for Dick Vermiel, one of the greatest guys ever in this game. And I'm happy he walked away from a terrific career. When Dick first took the Rams job three years ago after more than a decade out of coaching, I called to congratulate him and wish him well. He told me how mad his wife was at him. They had been planning a vacation in France for a couple of years, and his wife had been studying up for it. When Dick finally got up the courage to tell her there was a change in plans, he was taking the job, she was not very happy. Now they have the chance to go to France and do all the things they wanted to do. And go as champions.

I'm still not happy with Belichick. I don't know how you can take a million dollars to stay another year to become the head coach and then walk out on the job. Nothing he has said since about why it happened makes any sense to me.

But hopefully, we have made the most of the situation. I'm very happy with the way Al Groh has handled himself as head coach. I think our organization did a good job on the Keyshawn Johnson trade and using what we got in the draft to make the Jets a better team in the future.

The Keyshawn deal centered around his agent, Jerome Stanley, not one of my favorites. When Keyshawn made his original deal for six years with the Jets, it was before I got here. They gave him the biggest bonus ever at that point to get him on a six-year contract, so he wouldn't try to renegotiate at the end of three or four. Yet that is what happened. At the end of the third year, I tried to do something with the league to allow us to restructure his contract, not extend it, and they wouldn't let us do it. They said they would not approve the deal because it was in violation of the rules. We didn't agree with that, but there was nothing we could do.

Keyshawn's a terrific football player, and I like him very much as a person to this day. He's gone to Tampa, but I still like him a lot. At the end of his fourth year, the agent said he wanted to renegotiate. We told him this team has a rule about not renego-

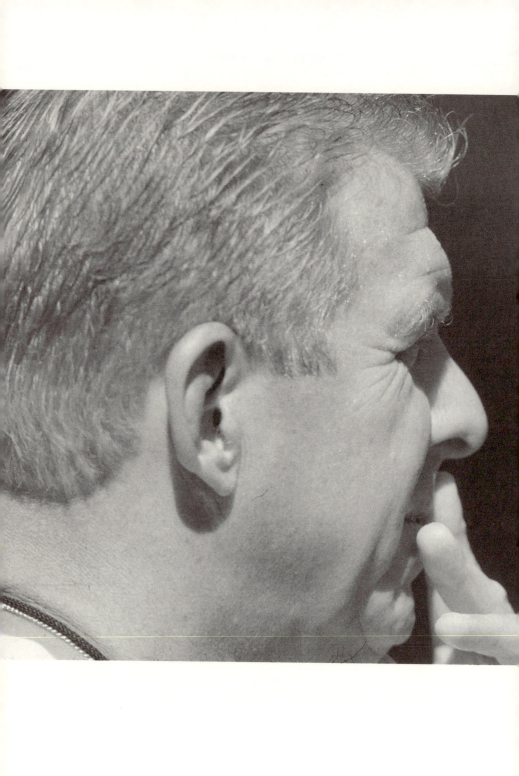

tiating a player's contract with two or more years left to go. The agent didn't want to listen to that.

So we—myself; Groh; our owner Mr. Johnson; Dick Haley, our director of personnel; and Mike Tannenbaum, our salary cap guy—considered our options. Here they were: we do nothing and end up with a bitter, probably disruptive player on our hands. We didn't have to let him go. We could have made him the franchise player and had him for the rest of his career. That was option one. The second was to renegotiate his contract, set a bad precedent, pay him a $12 million or $13 million bonus up front after our owner had just paid more than $600 million to buy the team. Also, if we did this, we would most likely have to let two or three of our good players go for salary cap reasons. The third option was the trade.

When we were at the league meetings the final week in March in Palm Beach, Rick McKay from Tampa told me they would give us their first two choices in the draft, both in the first round, for Keyshawn. There were a lot of rumors at the time about Baltimore making a deal, or Washington making a deal with us, but nothing ever really got serious with those two teams.

We talked about all these situations as a group, and all of the consequences that would come with each decision. In the end, even though we would have liked to keep him, Al decided the trade was the best way to go, and we all agreed with him.

We ended up with four picks in the first round as a result of the trade: our own, the one we got from New England for Belichick, and two from Tampa.

To me, the key to this whole deal is a quarterback we drafted in the first round, Chad Pennington out of Marshall. With Vinny's age, we would have had to go looking for another quarterback in the draft in a couple of years. And most times, it takes years to get lucky enough to get a chance to get a good one. If this kid becomes our quarterback for the future some- where down the road, then the Johnson trade is the kind of deal we'll make every time.

We picked a defensive lineman, Shaun Ellis of Tennessee, and a linebacker, John Abraham of South Carolina, as our first two draft selections. Ellis is the second best defensive lineman in the draft in our opinion, and Abraham, the third best linebacker. Both of them can rush the passer, and as you read throughout this book, we didn't have anyone who could rush the passer successfully on an individual basis. We feel both of these kids will be able to do that. Our final first-round pick was a tight end named Tony Becht of West Virginia. He has a chance to be the best two-way tight end the Jets have had for a long time.

In retrospect, a year ago we didn't have a first-round pick, and still did okay in the draft. Randy Thomas, our second pick, and Ryan Young, our seventh pick, should be two very good offensive lineman for us in years to come, and that is the position we had to deal with last year, so I have to give credit to our scouting department for the job they did.

Our general manager (that would be me) didn't have that great a year. Rick Mirer was a bad deal for us, and that was mine from start to finish. The free agents I signed, like Eric Green and Johnny Mitchell, were complete busts. Steve Atwater was okay, but not what I hoped he would be for us. All four of those guys are gone. Roman Phifer did a good job for us and should be pretty good for us the next few years.

Thankfully, Kevin Williams is going to come back. This kid came very close to dying on us last year. Somehow, I feel this whole experience is going to make him better. Our doctors told us that he almost died as a result of the throat infection after the Denver game. It was touch-and-go with him for a few days. He went from 195 pounds to 157 pounds in a matter of days. The doctors say he came close to going over the edge, and if he had, he never would have come back. It was something we could never seem to catch up with. We had the best doctors you could possibly have, and they got after it right away, but it seemed like we were always a half step behind trying to treat this thing. All the while that jerk he has for an agent, Stanley, the same guy who has Keyshawn, is yapping to the press that we were not doing the right thing by him. There were two other cases in the league similar to Kevin's last year, and we did a lot more for our player than the other two teams did for their player. The important thing is he's alive and well and has a chance to continue his career.

For the last four months, I have been trying to figure out what I'm going to do with the rest of my life. It hasn't been easy. I've had some very interesting and lucrative offers from television and the Internet, but right now, I think I'm going to stay with the Jets. There wasn't anything I have been offered that makes me want to leave at this time.

Now this is why I'm going to stay.

I put three years of hard work into this thing and I want to stay around and keep it going in the right direction.

I really like Al Groh a lot personally, and I want to stay around to help him. Whatever he asks me to do, wherever he wants me to help, I'll be available and he'll know that. But I'm not going to look over his shoulder. I didn't want anyone looking over mine, I'm not going to be over his.

I want to stay for this owner. I like Woody Johnson. He's a good guy and wants to do the right thing. I'd like to be with him a whole season, and sort of break him into the business, if that's what he would like me to do.

And I guess I must still love this game. No matter how much it killed me at times. No matter how frustrated I was last year. There are some things that happen on a team, especially a football team that goes through so much together, that doesn't happen anywhere else.

Right in the midst of the Belichick mess, just a few days after I retired as coach, I came back to my office late one night, and something caught my attention on my desk. I walked over and got a closer look, and it was a trophy. And with the trophy was a handwritten letter.

Dear Coach. This award means more to me than any award I have ever received. It means more to me than rushing titles, Pro

Bowls, the Rookie of the Year award I have. It's the most important award I have ever received. I want you to have it because you have given so much of yourself to the game, and to me. I love you—Boy Wonder.

Curtis Martin had just given me his Most Valuable Player award, given to him by his teammates. It is right at the top of the list of the most important awards I have ever been given.

—Bill Parcells, May 3, 2000

APPENDIX A
BILL PARCELLS: STATS

CAREER HONORS
SUPER BOWL XXI, XXV, WINNER

USA Today AFC Coach of the Year (1998)

Associated Press Coach of the Year (1994)

United Press International Coach of the Year (1994)

Maxwell Coach of the Year Award (1994)

USA Today AFC Coach of the Year (1994)

Pro Football Weekly Coach of the Year (1994)

Football Digest Coach of the Year (1994)

College and Pro Football Newsweekly AFC Coach of the Year (1994)

NFL Films Coach of the Year (1989)

Washington Post NFL Coach of the Year (1989)

NFL Coach of the Year (1986)

Pro Magazine NFC East Coach of the Year (1984)

REGULAR SEASON COACHING RECORD

		W	L	T	Pct
1983	Giants	3	12	1	.219
1984	Giants	9	7	0	.563
1985	Giants	10	6	0	.625
1986	Giants	14	2	0	.875
1987	Giants	6	9	0	.400
1988	Giants	10	6	0	.625
1989	Giants	12	4	0	.750
1990	Giants	13	3	0	.813
1993	Patriots	5	11	0	.313
1994	Patriots	10	6	0	.625
1995	Patriots	6	10	0	.375
1996	Patriots	11	5	0	.688
1997	Jets	9	7	0	.563
1998	Jets	12	4	0	.750
1999	Jets	8	8	0	.500
TOTALS		**138**	**100**	**1**	**.579**

POSTSEASON COACHING RECORD

		W	L	T	Pct
1984	Giants	1	1	0	.500
1985	Giants	1	1	0	.500
1986	Giants	3	0	0	1.000
1989	Giants	0	1	0	.000
1990	Giants	3	0	0	1.000
1994	Patriots	0	1	0	.000
1996	Patriots	2	1	0	.667
1998	Jets	1	1	0	.500
TOTALS		**11**	**6**	**0**	**.647**

APPENDIX B
THE 1999 NEW YORK JETS COACHING STAFF

When I first came to pro football with the New England Patriots twenty years ago, we had seven or eight coaches on the staff. Now we have twice as many, plus a support staff. As you'll see, every one of them has a crucial role to play.

What do I look for in a coach? I want someone who's consistent, who's not afraid to confront the players, and who makes the players accountable for their performance. A successful coach will not take excuses and is a very good teacher. There are a lot of different ways to communicate. What we have to do is find a way to teach the player what we want. No matter what it takes, we have to find the way to do it. There's a lot of different ways to skin a cat, so to speak, and we try to explore all of them.

OFFENSE

CHARLIE WEIS, OFFENSIVE COORDINATOR. He was a high school coach in New Jersey when I hired him with the Giants originally. He was recommended to me by Al Groh, the linebacker coach. He's a guy that Al knew very well. We gave him a few projects to do when we were first introduced to him as a tryout, and he did well in those areas. We decided to put him on the staff. His first year was the year we won the Super Bowl in 1990. I then took him to New England.

He coached both the tight ends and the wide receivers at New England. A year after we came to New York Ron Erhardt retired, and Charlie became the offensive coordinator.

DAN HENNING, QUARTERBACK/RECEIVERS COACH. Dan is a longtime friend who I coached at Florida State, where we first met back in 1969. He's a guy I've had a lot of respect for over the years. I think he's an outstanding quarterback/receiver combination coach. Dan has worked for Don Shula, Joe Gibbs, Walt Michaels. He's really got a vast array of pro experience and was the head coach for two different teams: the Atlanta Falcons and the San Diego Chargers. He did a magnificent job with Vinny Testaverde in 1998.

TODD HALEY, WIDE RECEIVERS COACH. Todd is a young guy who is under the wings of Weis and Henning. This is his first year as a position coach. He was an assistant to the offensive staff the year before, and he worked with the receivers on a part-time basis. This year he works with the receivers on a full-time basis.

PAT HODGSON, TIGHT ENDS COACH. Pat had been hired by Ray Perkins and was on our staff with the Giants for a number of years. He later went to Pittsburgh when they were in the Super Bowl against Dallas in 1994, with Ron Erhardt, who was our offensive coordinator with the Giants and later with the Jets my first year there. Pat wasn't at New England with us, but when I came to the Jets, he was already here. He also coached at the University of Georgia.

MAURICE CARTHON, OFFENSIVE BACKFIELD COACH. I gave Maurice his first job in professional football. He played running back for me with the Giants and in my second year with the Patriots. I think he's a bright, young guy that has a future as a head coach in the NFL. He was a very determined hard-working player, and he's proved to be the same as a coach. He gets very good results from the running backs.

BILL MUIR, OFFENSIVE LINE COACH. He was at the Jets when I arrived, and I retained him as a coach. I had known him somewhat from my interaction around the league, but he was highly recommended to me by Ron Erhardt and Pat Hodgson, who were coaches with the Jets that we kept. It worked out—he does an excellent job.

SPECIAL TEAMS

MIKE SWEATMAN, SPECIAL TEAMS COACH. He's been with me at all three places: the Giants, the Patriots, and the Jets. We hired Mike from the University of Kansas to be an assistant special teams coach with the Giants. Bill Belichick was our special teams coach back then, so Mike learned from Bill and then took over the job.

DEFENSE

BILL BELICHICK, ASSISTANT HEAD COACH, DEFENSIVE COORDINATOR. I first met Bill in 1981 with the Giants. He was the special teams coach when I was an assistant coach. He helped me on defense after I had become the head coach of the Giants. After the second year, I named him defensive coordinator. He stayed with me through the 1990 season. Then he became the head coach at the Cleveland Browns. He was fired by the Browns after the 1995 season and we hired him at the Patriots in 1996. He became the interim head coach for the Jets, and then when I took the head coach job with the Jets, he became assistant head coach. He has been around football all of his life. His father had coached at the Naval Academy for many years. He is an astute football guy. He is good with the Xs and Os and has done an excellent job for me over the years.

AL GROH, LINEBACKERS COACH. I know Al from our college days at West Point in the 1960s. He was a freshman coach when I was on the varsity staff. He was head coach at Wake Forest. Then I helped him get a job with Marion Campbell at the Atlanta Falcons. He went to South Carolina for a year, and we then hired him at the Giants in the late 1980s. He's a good teacher, very energetic, very bright.

ROMEO CRENNEL, DEFENSIVE LINE COACH. Romeo has been with me longer than anyone. We coached together in college at Texas back in the mid–1970s. He then came to the Giants as an assistant special teams coach when I was an assistant coach, on my recommendation to Ray Perkins. Then he went on to be the head special teams coach of the Giants and eventually to the defensive line. Through all the years with the Giants, Patriots, and Jets, Romeo has been with me.

ERIC MANGINI, DEFENSIVE QUALITY CONTROL COACH. Eric was hired by Bill Belichick when he was the interim coach. He helps the defensive staff in their scouting, does the breakdowns of the opponents in advance, and does all of the peripheral jobs in terms of research and preparation for practice. He's really a defensive assistant with no specific coaching assignment. He does a lot of the paperwork, a lot of the preparation for practice in terms of the schedules and the cards that we use to show the plays on the field. Basically he's a jack-of-all-trades. Whatever needs to be done to help the staff, he does.

OTHER

CARL BANKS, PLAYER DEVELOPMENT. One of the first things I did when I arrived at the Jets is hire Carl, one of my old Giants players. I took some flak for that because some people felt I should take a former Jet. If I knew one that was better than Carl I would have. But Carl, in my opinion, was the best man I could get for what I wanted. Carl knows what it is like to play and live in New York. It's a lot different from Mississippi, or some of the places these kids come from. A lot of these guys are hillbillies in a sense, and they think that just because they're in New York they're smart and handsome. I want Carl there to meet them when they come to town and take them through a period of orientation. He can recommend where to live, where to bank, basically where to go and where not to go. He is available to talk to the players at all times.

CLAY HAMPTON, EQUIPMENT MANAGER. Clay was with the Jets since before I arrived. His father was the equipment man for many years and now he has taken over.

DAVID PRICE, HEAD TRAINER. David was with the Jets when I got here. He came from the Philadelphia Eagles and he's an outstanding trainer with a tremendous work ethic. He rehabilitates the players extensively. He's one of the few guys who takes the players right from the team plane in the middle of the night to the training room to give them treatment so that their injuries don't have a chance to worsen while the player sleeps on them at night.

JOHN LOTT, STRENGTH COACH. We lost our strength coach when we left New England, so we searched the college ranks and found John, who came highly recommended from the University of Houston. I'm always concerned about hiring people from faraway places, particularly from the South or the Southwest, and bringing them to New York, because it's a culture shock for them. Lots of times they have trouble adjusting, but John's done a good job and he's intense at heart. He is a very hard worker and works personally with the players at great length. He does a lot of the running conditioning with them as they do it. I think he's done a good job for us.

STEVE YARNELL, DIRECTOR OF SECURITY. Steve played football for me when I coached at West Point back in the 1960s. He was with the FBI for twenty-three years before retiring. He has many jobs, including arranging security for team travel, arranging transportation, and when these guys get in trouble with the law off the field, and some of them will, they see Steve. Not me.

ACKNOWLEDGMENTS

Thanks to Steve Gutman, Frank Ramos, and the entire New York Jets staff. And thanks to Alec Radzikowski of Boston for his assistance with the book.